The
Soul's Journey
Into
God's Embrace

Terry Wardle

Sandberg Leadership Center

THE SOUL'S JOURNEY INTO GOD'S EMBRACE

FIRST EDITION
Copyright © 2000 by
Terry Wardle

Library of Congress Control Number: 00-132241

ISBN 0-7880-1631-8

PRINTED IN U.S.A.

Other Books by Terry Wardle

Whispers of Love in Seasons of Fear

Draw Close to the Fire: Finding God in the
Darkness

Wounded: How to Find Wholeness and Inner
Healing Through Him

One to One: A Practical Guide to Friendship
Evangelism

Exalt Him: Designing Dynamic Worship Services

Dedication

To Aaron, my son.
A man after God's own heart.

Table Of Contents

Foreword

I first met Terry Wardle at an interview for an upcoming faculty position at Ashland Theological Seminary. As I sat in the meeting, I was deeply impressed with both his outer and inner presence. I knew he was a person who had been tested by fire and been refined in the process.

Terry spoke to us of the core values that were at the heart of what he was all about as a Christian minister and educator. He shared that he was committed to excellence in teaching, but teaching that grew from the heart. He assured us that he sought to combine scholarship with spiritual formation in a way that would lay a foundation for well being in the lives of students. He spoke confidently and with a passion that told me there was more to him than was on the surface. He spoke from experience. Within weeks we brought Terry back to campus to meet with our entire faculty, who gave a unanimous vote to offer the position to Terry. The rest is history.

Terry's underlying passion is to *find out what God is doing and become part of it*. And passion it is. He often thinks outside the box and then invites everyone along for the journey. His newest book, *The Soul's Journey Into God's Embrace*, encourages Christians of all ages to join in an exciting journey toward intimacy with God. In this book, Terry helps connect us with the divine presence of God.

This is a practical book. Its beauty is found in its emphasis upon a community of faith that is supportive and celebrative.

You will feel yourself let go of many old wounds, hurts and disappointments. Somehow, as you move forward to the wonder of God's love, they lose their power and significance.

I am pleased that Terry has chosen to have this book published under the auspices of The Sandberg Leadership Center. Ashland Theological Seminary has launched this new center with the grids of spiritual formation and leadership intersecting with academic excellence. The Sandberg Leadership Center is dedicated to reaching segments of leadership throughout our society by impacting them with a value-oriented, character-forming model of leadership. This will be a refreshing approach that is critical for our churches as well as for the communities we serve. All around we are hearing the cry for effective leadership. Not a leadership that has all the answers, but a leadership that makes a difference. *The Soul's Journey Into God's Embrace* touches the heart of what we are about in shaping leaders to meet the growing needs of our changing society and world.

There are many lessons we can all learn from *The Soul's Journey Into God's Embrace* and I encourage you to start the journey of discovery.

Frederick J. Finks, President
Ashland Theological Seminary

Introduction

It was a clear morning in the mountains of Pennsylvania, with deep snow covering the frozen ground outside. It was bone-chilling cold, and the ice that covered the windows was a warning to stay inside by the warm fire. Yet, I stood at the door of the rustic cabin fully dressed, hardly able to wait to get into the forest. I had been anticipating this day for a long time, and the frigid weather was not going to spoil the moment. I was thirteen years old and about to embark on my first and long anticipated deer hunt.

Cousins, uncles, and family friends were all gathered in my Uncle Ray's hunting lodge, a tradition that had been observed for years. I had heard of this almost mystical place many times through the stories and family lore that surrounded the annual trip to the big woods. Children were not permitted to attend the yearly rendezvous, only men. But at thirteen everything changed, and I was soon to experience one of the most important days of my young life. Why? Because I was about to finally become one of them, a true hunter. Where I grew up, becoming a woodsman was no less a right of passage than the vision quest of a young Native American or the calling into manhood ceremonies of the Mandingo of West Africa. It was my moment, and I was not going to miss it because of a little bad weather.

I was excited and full of energy, even though I had not slept a wink all night. Laughter, tall tales and the snoring of sleeping men kept me wide awake through the long hours before the dawn. Breakfast was over and as daylight broke through the darkness, anticipation was high. We hurriedly gathered outside camp to receive final instructions for the day. Decisions about hunting buddies and rendezvous times were communicated. A lot of teasing and bragging was in the air, as well as good natured fun. I loved every bit of it, and had waited too long to miss out on anything. It was a dream come true.

Just before leaving for the woods attention was drawn to a large iron bell mounted on the outside corner of the old barn. It had been placed there years earlier as a safeguard for every hunter in that small valley. The mountains of north-western Pennsylvania are marked by vast stretches of hard-wood forest. And as my dad repeatedly told me, it is very easy to get disoriented. It had happened before, often re-sulting in great harm to those who had lost their way. And it could easily happen again. We were told that if evening came and any one of us did not come in, we needed to listen for the sound of the bell. It would be rung over and over, until the one who was lost made it home, safe again.

Thankfully, as a boy I never did lose my way in the Penn-sylvania woods. Unfortunately, I was not as lucky in man-hood. For over two decades I have walked the sometimes dangerous terrain of Christian ministry. Be assured, it is an exciting and privileged place to spend a life. But the ever-changing landscape of spiritual and emotional highs and lows can be disorienting. This is especially true when a per-son spends all his time with his head down working, never stopping to find out where he is. It is possible to get misdi-rected and lost ... very lost. And that is exactly what hap-pened to me. I cannot describe the pain and heartache that resulted, a memory of darkness and cold night that still pierces to the deepest regions of my soul. Loneliness and fear were overwhelming, as well as the desperate feeling that I may not find my way back to home, ever again.

But God knew where I was all the time and like a bell ringing through the coldest night, He kept calling out, beckoning me to come home to His embrace. When I finally stopped running I heard the sound of His love-filled voice, and it brought hope to my troubled heart. The Father was compassionately calling me to come back to Himself, to the place of rest and peace. Battered and badly bruised, I began to make my way toward His embrace, well aware that I was being strengthened and encouraged by the Holy Spirit each step along the way.

That season of despair and sadness was a hard way to learn a fundamental lesson of the Christian life. You and I were made to experience and enjoy intimacy with our Heavenly Father. It is the very center of life. I am not talking about simply a theological understanding of His love, but an experiential reality. It is a gift of His grace, available to every believer through Jesus Christ. Being daily in His presence is to be the source of your strength, your place of direction, your very purpose for life. Only there will you find the peace and joy and fulfillment you so desperately desire. Nothing, not even Christian ministry, should keep you from the continual journey to the warmth of His loving embrace.

Forget this and you are all too suddenly in harm's way. When you get so busy that you fail to center in Him, it is all too easy to lose direction, get disoriented, discouraged or destroyed. And unfortunately, far too many Christians are unknowingly risking their own well-being because they fail to fellowship with Him regularly.

I often wonder if we are like the Ephesian believers spoken of in the book of Revelation, chapter 2:1-7. We are hard-working, fighting evil in society, testifying to Christ around the world, and at times enduring trial and hardship. But like these early Christians, are we possibly in danger of wandering from our first love? Have we become so preoccupied with the cares of ministry that we have forgotten the strength and delight of having meaningful com-munion and fellowship with God? As a result, are we not often tired, ineffective, and on the verge of burnout? Thankfully, our heavenly Father loves us dearly and is calling out, inviting us to find rest and peace in the wonder of His loving presence.

This is a book about the soul's journey to God's embrace. It is written as an effort to help you understand the spiritual and practical dynamics of growing ever closer to Him. In no way do I believe it is *the* answer to building a meaningful relationship with the Triune God. It is simply an attempt, meager as it may be, to motivate and guide you in investing the time of your life in knowing Him. If you do you will find that it leads to the most satisfying, fulfilling and transforming relationship imaginable. While seasons of heartache, trial and hardship will still be an ever-present reality, you will discover that He is present with you, even when you do not know it, to bring peace and strength to your life. And what is better yet, you will find that it is but the beginning. For knowing God and Jesus, His Son, is what life is all about, both now and forever.

"Now this is eternal life: That they may know you, the only true God, and Jesus Christ, whom you have sent" (John 17:3).

I want to express special thanks to the fellow pilgrims who helped me with this book. My wife Cheryl told me it was time to write this and encouraged me each step along the way. My son Aaron read each rough draft and inspired me to keep going in spite of difficulty. My daughters, Cara and Emily, were constant channels of love and grace, as well as my precious daughter-in-law Destry. John Shultz, Linda Hartzfeld, Anne Halley and Judy Allison are faithful friends who believed and encouraged me through the final stages of writing. And finally to Peter and Pam Burgo, who gave me a quiet place to wrestle with this book. May God bless you all, and thanks.

Special thanks to Louise Waller for original art and cover design. I encourage you to take time and reflect upon the insert on the front cover. At first you will notice that the painting is of a cloud-filled sky. But if you set your imagination free you may just see something more. Or Someone.

Chapter One

The Joy Of The Journey

As the spring of 1992 drew to a close, I began a terrifying decent into a debilitating dark night. Having spent two decades in Christian ministry, I was reaping an unpleasant harvest gathered from years of overwork and a performance-based approach to ministry. What began as ever increasing seasons of anxiety ultimately led to deep depression and a frightening bout with agoraphobia. I felt terribly lost and without help or hope.

For months I battled these symptoms alone, afraid that rejection and disqualification would result from any serious attempts to get help. Finally, in desperation, I admitted myself into a Christian psychiatric hospital. Unable to function as I once had, it was necessary that I submit to professional care. What followed were months of recovery and a total reshaping of my understanding regarding what true and balanced ministry is all about. While I had accomplished much in my career, I had grown tired, barren and at risk deep within. The onset of a very dark time helped me see what I had been blinded to for so long. The soul's journey to God's embrace must be first and foremost in the life of every Christian. Only in His arms is there the acceptance, strength and life required to make it through. My hope is that by addressing the importance of this issue you will be excited and empowered to move daily toward God's intimate and loving heart.

What Happens When You Pursue Intimacy With God?

The benefits and blessings that flow from being in the Father's presence are inexhaustible. Your very life can be transformed. Soaking before Him in adoration, devotion, and meditation will bring you peace, comfort in times of trouble, joy, insight, and strength for service, as well as countless other blessings. These riches are not for select super Christians, but for every person who humbly enters the Father's presence, including you and me.

Unfortunately, most of us are missing the Treasure hunt of a lifetime. Far too many of God's precious children are caught in a destructive pattern of life that will ultimately leave them empty and disillusioned. The demands of daily life, busy schedules and countless preoccupations keep Christians from resting in the Presence that brings meaning and joy to life. It is as if we, who were meant to feast in His presence, are satisfied with crumbs, often unaware that a rich table has been spread before us.

For many, there has been inadequate teaching about the journey to God's embrace. Christianity has all too often been based upon conforming one's behavior to some acceptable standard, and understanding certain theological principles. Discipleship seems to be about not drinking, or smoking or, God forbid, dancing. Rules and regulations become the focal point of Christian life. Intimacy, if mentioned at all, is relegated to a concept of faith, not an experiential reality. Many Christians are desperately thirsty for more, yet unaware that there is even living water to drink.

Your heavenly Father has made a way for you to experience the wonder of His embrace. Through faith in Jesus Christ you are positioned to draw near to His presence and taste of a divinely set banquet. The rich fare offers blessings that will constantly change you at the deepest level of life. It is a feast that you are not just to gaze upon, read about, or imagine. It is to be consumed with joy as you come to the table of His love. Consider just a few of these gifts, allowing the discussion to quicken a deep desire to move into the celebration of His embrace.

Peace and Rest

Centuries ago Augustine wrote that human beings would find no rest until they found it in God. Having tried the sensuous and intellectual pleasures of this world, he discovered that the love of the Father singularly and completely satisfied his deepest hunger. Augustine wrote of this in his poem, *Late Have I Loved Thee.*

> *Late have I loved thee, O beauty so ancient and so new, late have I loved Thee! And Behold, Thou wert within and I was without. I was looking for Thee out there, and I threw myself, deformed as I was upon those well-formed things which Thou hast made. Thou wert with me, yet I was not with Thee. These things held me far from Thee, things which would not have existed had they not been in Thee. Thou didst call and cry out and burst in upon my deafness; Thou didst shine forth and glow and drive away my blindness; thou didst send forth Thy fragrance, and I drew my breath, and now I pant for Thee; I have tasted, and now I hunger and thirst; Thou didst touch me, and I was inflamed with desire for Thy peace.*

Sight! Panting for God! Catching the fragrance of His love! Inflamed for Him! What wonderful, power-filled images of a passionate relationship with God. This is the Reality that your Father offers if you dare to draw near. Your Christian life is to be alive with such love and peace. How sad, how inadequate, how incomplete is the notion that faith is only about belief and behavior. Being a Christian is your opportunity to be ignited by the flame of His presence and to be satisfied deep within by nothing less than God Himself.

Augustine knew that there is within every person an emptiness that is only filled by pursuing a personal relationship with God. Being born again does not, in itself, satisfy this hunger for fulfillment. It does give birth to Kingdom life, which endows Christians with the potential for a meaningful union with the Father through Jesus Christ. Unfortunately, many never invest in this passionate pursuit and as a result the inner restlessness persists, often leading to a destructive drivenness. Striving and performing have become epidemic in Christian communities, as if busyness somehow solidifies our status with God and identifies us as mature followers of Christ.

Walter was experiencing almost debilitating depression. He had experienced a less than satisfying stay at an in-patient recovery program. He had been properly medicated there, but did not agree with the direction counseling had taken him. Believing he needed to address spiritual factors, Walter sought out spiritual direction.

His story was certainly heartbreaking, yet not all that unfamiliar. He had just retired from forty years of pastoral ministry, which included starting numerous local churches, shaping denominational mission strategies and ably serving in national church leadership. Throughout his ministry, Walter worked incessantly, twice to the point of hospitalization. For years he carried two and three responsibilities at a time, even at the risk of personal health and family well-being. Walter was, for many, a model of a man who gave it all for Jesus.

But retirement was to expose a serious problem in Walter's motivation. Now that the "work" had stopped, he seemed to have come up empty. There was a deep dissatisfaction and apparent meaningless to life that led him to despair. This, as well as an economic crisis, brought this man of action to a screeching halt.

Walter revealed to his caregiver that all throughout his ministry, he took little time to fellowship with God. His energies were singularly devoted to service. He said that when he was working he experienced personal fulfillment. But as soon as a task reached its conclusion, another had to be within reach or unrest would begin to surface. Nervous dissatisfaction would press Walter to pursue yet another service-related goal.

Walter had done it all. But when it came to knowing God, he admittedly had barely taken his first step. He was 65 years old, tired, emotionally ill and without a clue as to where to begin. But to the Lord's praise, once Walter recognized this imbalance it opened the way to a new and much healthier life. Repenting and renouncing performance as a means of fulfillment, Walter set out to experience God. And God met him.

Like the father in the parable of the prodigal, Walter encountered God rushing toward him with great healing love. He was amazed to find that joy and acceptance flooded his soul, as well as a deep peace and understanding. Walter had returned home and the fire of God's presence satisfied like nothing had before in his life. He finally found what he was looking for, and there was rest.

Comfort In Difficulty

No one likes pain. But as discomforting and debilitating as it is, pain serves a very important purpose in your life. It is, if you will, a messenger trying to get your attention, warning you that something is wrong. But when the alarm sounds, instead of seeking God's help in going after the root problem, people try to kill the messenger. And the painkillers of choice include many sinful and addictive behaviors that may provide short-term relief, but invariably bring ultimate destruction. Drug addiction, sexual misconduct, eating disorders, workaholism, gambling and many other coping mechanisms all serve to kill pain. Many Christians readily identify such actions as wrong and unhealthy. However, at the same time they are often caught in any one of several "socially acceptable" addictions, like overeating, hours in front of the television, too much sleep, obsessive shopping and the like. Such behaviors never really touch the cause of the pain itself, leaving it to further infect and debilitate people's lives.

What does God desire of you when trial and pain sets in? The Bible repeatedly says that the Lord longs to show compassion to His hurting children. He wants you to turn to Him when you hurt, to invite Him into the difficult place and then receive His help. Sometimes He will give you strength to endure the trial as a pathway to growth. Often He will open a way of deliverance and emotional healing. Invariably He offers you the mysterious power of His presence, that in just being "there" you find a comfort that brings hope and rest. Assuredly He does not want you to feel alone, abandoned or rejected. He beckons you to draw near to His intimate embrace and experience the power of His love.

Anne Halley, a friend and gifted caregiver, recently spent time with a man who felt the pain of rejection when an organization he had worked with told him they were no longer comfortable with his spiritual journey. They felt he was becoming too charismatic, and as a result, they would no longer be supporting his ministry. Their response hurt, causing him to experience mild depression. Anne encouraged him not to throw himself into work or some other behavior to kill the pain. Instead, she challenged him to press into the Father's presence, to wait before Him in all the pain. Anne asked him to tell God how he felt about the rejection, and ask for the Lord's touch and insight. At first he was uncomfortable with the idea. But he eventually followed the advice and returned saying that the encounter with God was so profound that he almost wanted to bless the pain that took him there in the first place. The hurt actually drew him closer to his Lord and his love.

Turning to God, not to sinful and painful addictions, is the proper response to emotional pain. Whether it be with the help of a trusted caregiver, or alone, taking your hurts and difficulties to the Lord is the path to personal wholeness. Doing this not only deals with the pain, it enhances a growing relationship with Him, which is the treasure of life.

Struggling through an issue before the Lord actually helps you know Him better. Experiencing His love, compassion and healing touch when you hurt ignites an increased hunger for even deeper intimacy.[1] You discover that He is in fact good and cares so very much just for you. In the end, the object of your greatest pain can become the doorway to your most meaningful relationship in life.

The Christian Life Comes Alive

All across the United States people are leaving churches because they are not being connected with the presence of God. While programs and causes abound, the experience of that divine *mysterium tremendum* is just not there. Being part of a local church is, in such cases, not much different from being part of a social service organization. Committee work and lifeless ritual become the marks of involvement. Tired and disillusioned, people are now exiting the church in large numbers.

This does not just happen in theologically liberal congregations. It occurs anywhere and everywhere church leaders fail to connect people with God's divine presence. Jesus came to give people what they need most, a relationship with their Heavenly Father that is real and life-transforming. It is just such a relationship that enlivens and empowers the Christian experience. Without it, church life becomes either duty without life or an exercise in endurance. This can be true even where God's word is faithfully proclaimed, if and when knowing the word preempts growing closer to the Lord.

God's presence, through the Holy Spirit, brought life and joy to early Christians even in times of trial and suffering. There was an air of anticipation and expectation that fueled their faith. They never knew what kind of exciting encounter they were to experience when they came together in the name of Jesus Christ. People were healed, demons would flee, and men and women would lay down their very possessions in response to the Father's love. Some people dramatically fell dead before the Lord, while others supernaturally came back

21

to life. Bored in church? Never! In risk of falling asleep in church? You must be kidding! These early believers found life inside the church more exciting than anything the world could offer.

Is that kind of Christian experience just a thing of the past? Not at all. Your God is still moving in the world in ways that defy explanation. Far from distant and inactive, He is visiting people all around the globe with exciting encounters in His presence. God still whispers words of love to those who draw near, continues to satisfy hungry hearts, and works daily to provide, heal, empower and direct anyone willing to come in faith. The Christian life is exciting and transforming when lived in His embrace.

Do you desire such a relationship with the living God? It is clear that He desires that level of relationship with you, for Jesus came for that express purpose. Connect with His heart and, frankly, there will be no holding you back. Christianity is about knowing a "Person." Prioritizing intimacy with God unites you with the one Life that always begets life! When that happens the Christian life is vibrant and fully inspired. In the following chapters you will discover specific and practical principles that will help position you for the most exciting journey of your life.

Discernment

One of the most important questions you can ask is, "What is God doing and how am I to respond?" Knowing the answer to this question demands an ever-growing relationship with God. Jesus was healing people on the Sabbath and this infuriated the religious community of His day. Enraged, they not only persecuted Christ, they sought to kill Him. Why? Because Jesus was breaking the rules. And devotion to rules was what religious life was all about for Israel's leaders. In their eyes, anyone who violated the religious law was certainly not of God.

Jesus, however, did not make his ministry choices based on rules, but instead out of His relationship with the Heavenly Father. When questioned about why He did the things he did, Jesus made a statement that is the key to all effective ministry. He said,

> I tell you the truth, the Son can do nothing by Himself; He can do only what He sees His Father doing, because whatever the Father does, the Son does also. For the Father loves the Son and shows Him all He does.
>
> —John 5:19, 20

Christ's love relationship with God the Father was foundational to His ministry. Repeatedly in scripture we see our Lord getting apart to commune with God. He found places of solitude where he sought the Father's love, direction and empowerment. One with God, Jesus was able to discern what the Father was doing and participated with Him. Relationship enabled Jesus to work in perfect harmony with the Kingdom and made Him effective in service to broken and lost people.

Why should you prioritize the journey to God's embrace? In addition to what has already been mentioned, it will enhance discernment in your life. You are not to be out doing just anything and everything in ministry. This leads only to frustration and ineffectiveness. The key to meaningful ministry is doing what the Father is doing, moving in the stream of His presence and divine activity. Many Christians decide to do something, and then pray for God to bless their efforts. It is as if people ask God to approve the final product of their own design without having waited to discern His purposes. The Lord demonstrated in His own life that it is far better first to discern His activity and then participate with Him. God is always at work, and you must learn to move out in harmony with His ministry.

This approach to ministry demands discernment, and discernment comes through relationship. In John 5:19, quoted previously, we read that Jesus said that God loved Him and as a result showed Him what to do. By pursuing an ever-increasing intimacy with God you will be able to harvest the fruit of this Christ-like approach to ministry. Yet as you do, you will find service and ministry taking on a whole new power and effectiveness. Grow in your relationship with God, and ministry no longer takes on a hit-and-miss quality that is frustrating and in some cases futile. You, through pursuing a dynamic relationship with Christ, can impact the world for Him. It is not dependent on man-made programs and strategies, as it is intimate prayer and time in His glorious embrace. In His presence you will gain the insight needed to move with God, where God is already active ... and there exciting things begin to happen.

Strength in Ministry

Our world is glutted with needs. Broken, lost and hurting people are everywhere. While the human condition may be more noticeable on the streets of New York or neighborhoods of East L. A., no community is without opportunities for ministry far greater than our capacity to provide help. Most of God's people are eager to do their part in obedience to Christ, sometimes with an unhealthy result.

Burn-out in ministry is almost epidemic. Pastors, missionaries and Christian laypeople are giving of themselves until it literally hurts them. They work long hours, accommodate their schedules to the needs of countless people and often ignore basic principles of well being. As a result, centers of rest and renewal are springing up all over the country. The issue is real and the need great, as more and more of God's servants break under the pressures of ministry.

Having "been there" myself, and after working with scores of people in similar straits, I am concerned that the absence of intimacy with God lies at the core. Unconnected with God, servants lack discernment (as already stated), the empowerment of His presence and the healing ministry that always comes from time with Him. People are left to operate in the power of the flesh, which is totally incapable of enduring the demands of ministry. They often are unable to say no and seldom take time to fill the reserves of their own lives. Ultimately, the toll is too great and God's people are forced to shut down lest they die. And regardless of the noble portrait one tries to paint, this type of death does not bring glory to God.

Jesus said that His "yoke is easy and His burden light." He desires to infuse you with His strength to accomplish the tasks He designs and directs. And He intends for you to be regularly strengthened and healed in the warm light of His presence. In His intimate embrace care and healing come. You do not have to live the Christian life in your own strength and power. God is to be your source, offering an exciting servanthood that comes only through relationship with Him.

Why then are so many collapsing under the load? I believe there are two reasons such breakdowns occur. First, some dear people are endeavoring to carry the Lord's burden in their own strength. They have not yet learned how to receive His promised empowerment for the task. And secondly, there are far too many Christians wearing a yoke Jesus never intended for them. Whether of their own or someone else's making, they are working apart from the Lord's true purpose for their lives. Both of these improper approaches to ministry come at a great cost and ultimately lead to personal disaster.

You were made to soak in the presence of God. There, He waits to meet you and empower, enlighten and care for you. He intends for His love and embrace to overflow into service that is effective and efficient. Yes, there is a cost to discipleship and a sacrificial nature to service. But the price need not include poor health, emotional turmoil and the neglect of family. Where the Lord calls, He promises to provide. When He gives vision, His provision follows. And all of this and much more awaits you in the wonder of His glorious embrace.

A Tragic Absence Of Intimacy

Let's face the truth. As exciting as the prospect of intimacy is, it is far too easy for Christians to major in what is

25

less important, while missing the heart of what salvation truly offers. Many evangelicals prioritize evangelism and mission, investing great amounts of time and resource in winning the world for Christ. Christians who embrace a more liberal theology often focus most on social action and humanitarian aid, expending their energies in relieving the pain of the suffering millions. The seminary and college community can consider academic inquiry as of utmost importance to the Christian life, seeking to equip men and women to change the world by prioritizing knowledge above all else. Countless charismatics emphasize spiritual power and supernatural encounters as the ultimate experience of the Christian faith.

Be assured I am not saying these matters are unimportant. They are critical tools and tasks of the Christian life, part of the commission of Christ for His people and are to be embraced with a sense of urgency. But they must *never* replace intimacy with God as the ultimate pursuit of the life of faith. It is not zeal for a cause that ignites a world for God, but an ever-growing passion for intimacy. Broken and lost people are not waiting for a sermon, hungry for a Sunday school class, nor desperately crying out for a new program from the church. People need Jesus, and in the deepest part of their inner self they are longing for a touch from Him. If you intend to offer Christ to the world in a way that is meaningful and relevant, you must give time and energy to growing in relationship with Him. Apart from that, only imbalance and spiritual ill health result.

Thankfully, in recent years there has been increasing attention given to the critical issues of devotion and spiritual life. It is exciting to see an ever-growing body of literature being made available that inspires and informs people to experience God afresh. It is particularly hopeful that various Christian colleges and seminaries are taking serious steps to integrate spirituality into campus and curricular life. I've also been blessed to see several para-church ministries offering local and regional seminars on the topic of prayer and spiritual development. But the fact remains that the vast majority of us have yet to translate all this information into concerted effort to prioritize devotional intimacy above all else.

A Prophetic Moment

The staff meeting at Doug Collier's church began each week with a light breakfast, followed by ten to fifteen minutes of prayer and then business. For the most part, times together were both productive and good fun. But more than once it had been suggested that they give more serious attention to prayer. In part it was because they thought they needed it, and to another degree it grew out of the conviction that prayer should be a preoccupation for people in vocational ministry. At one point, the staff even went so far as to set aside an afternoon a week for just that purpose. But quite frankly it was difficult getting everyone there at the same time. The demands of ministry seemed always to give reason for one or two people not to attend.

It appeared as though this one Wednesday morning was to be like any other, with the staff anticipating business as usual. But as Doug described it to me, an ambush set by the Lord dramatically changed that day's agenda. The pastoral staff had bowed for the normal time of prayer, characterized by silence from some and sincerity by most. Suddenly, Rick, the pastor to single adults, began to cry. He started softly, but in just a few moments he was weeping almost uncontrollably. Everyone's attention naturally focused on him. A couple of people drew to his side, each placing a hand of care and encouragement on his shoulder. Others stayed seated, yet were supportive and concerned.

After a few moments, Judy, minister to women at the church, broke in, asking Rick to share what was going on with him. Doug told me that his words were penetrating and unforgettable. Rick said, "It seems as though I am experiencing the Lord's heart. It's a deep sorrow and I can't stop crying. I think it is about us. I hear Him asking, 'Why must I bring you to the place of brokenness before you draw near to me?' I sense the Lord's longing to spend time with us, yet it's as if He is saying we are too busy to come near."

More tears began to flow, but this time Rick was not the only one crying. Several people began to confess openly that they had not been pursuing ever-deepening communion with the Lord. Others, who had already begun to prioritize intimacy in their lives, knew that the Lord was wanting even more. Before that meeting ended, everyone was convinced that God was beckoning them to invest in the journey to His embrace like never before. This happened during the final days of Doug's ministry with that particular congregation. But while still there he could see that this encounter ran deep and began to bear significant fruit in the lives of each staff member there that day. And it began to affect the priorities of the congregation as well. Pursuing God more intentionally became the heart cry of countless people in the local church, and rightly so.

This prophetic moment with one church staff represents the heart of the Lord for His entire body. There are over two billion people on this planet who profess faith in Christ. And my experience is admittedly limited to a barely measurable fraction of that number. But if it is at all indicative of the broader Christian community, countless believers are finding it difficult to pursue intimacy with God in their daily lives. Busy in Christian service, many do not stop to commune with their Father in heaven, the central privilege of being His children. Others just don't realize that there is more available in their relationship with the Lord. But neither you nor I need spend one moment more in that dry place. The Father is calling. Will you begin the journey home to His arms of love?

Questions For Discussion And Review

1. How would you describe your relationship with the Lord?

Growing. If so, in what ways?

Stagnate. If so, why?

Distancing. If so, what effect is this having on your life?

2. What are your priorities in life? List them below in order of importance.

3. Are you investing time and resources in your priorities? If so, detail how you are and if not, why?

4. Do your priorities align with what you believe the Bible teaches?

5. In what practical ways do you pursue intimacy with God?

6. People who fail to invest in building an intimate relationship with God often experience any one or more of the following. On a scale of 1-5, to what degree do you find these in your life?

	Little				Much
Drivenness	1	2	3	4	5
Addictive Behaviors	1	2	3	4	5
Lifeless Christianity	1	2	3	4	5
Lack of Discernment	1	2	3	4	5
Fatigue and Burn-out	1	2	3	4	5

7. What is God's antidote for each of the above?

8. Would you be willing to stop and pray, asking God to help you journey to His embrace above all else? If your answer is yes, there is no better time to do it than right now. If no, why?

Chapter Two

Invitation To The Journey

It had been my privilege to meet each Thursday evening with a dozen Christian men and women for mutual encouragement and support. Most were people deeply involved in leadership at various local churches, including several people in full time vocational ministry. Everyone there had been experiencing significant levels of difficulty and trial, and they were trying to move beyond the pain and heartache to a more balanced and stable life. The one common conviction of every participant was that the answer for us all was to be found in the Lord Jesus Christ.

It was my role to facilitate our evenings together, part of my responsibilities with Spring Meadow Retreat Center. Spring Meadow was established as a place of renewal and restoration for broken and burned-out Christians. Thursday evening meetings had been designed as a time for worship, a brief scriptural challenge, sharing and, most importantly, individual prayer ministry.

One particular evening I was talking quite openly about developing an ever-growing relationship with our Heavenly Father. I shared with my friends the conviction that the proper response to difficulty and trial is certainly not insisting upon a way of escape. I know that is the normal first reaction to difficulty, but not the best. Instead, I told them that God's children are to offer painful times to the Lord as a means of growing in greater intimacy with Him, which is the privilege and priority of the Christian experience, the Treasure which makes all else pale in comparison. I assured them that dark times, though truly painful, held the possibility of opening their eyes to His love and affection in a way nothing else could. I knew this would be hard for them to understand, as it was for me. But it was a truth that could set them free as little else.

At what seemed like the high point of my presentation, Scott, a pastor from the area, interrupted. He looked intently into my eyes and said, "Terry, I've heard you speak about this before, and it all sounds so good. I've wanted this kind of relationship with all my heart. But frankly, I've tried to get there and it just doesn't happen. That has deeply hurt and bothered me. I feel like something is wrong with me or that I can't have it. Honestly, I avoid the pain and frustration by just concentrating on serving Him."

Before I could speak another person responded. "I'm with you, Scott. People talk about intimacy with God, but I've never experienced it. I've come to believe it's for some special people God chooses, but not average Christians like me. It just isn't there."

These responses may not be far from your own feelings about pursuing intimacy with the Lord. Like most Christians, you probably believe it is important to life, yet may conclude such a relationship is not really possible, at least not for you. Unhealthy, wooden attempts at devotional life may have discouraged you, causing you to believe that such a pursuit is fruitless in the long run. This, as well as other definable obstacles, can lead to the unbiblical and unreal conclusion that experiences of intimacy with the Lord will not come to you on this side of heaven. But I assure you this is not true. Deeper experiences in His presence do await you, and the pathway to that embrace can be found.

The greater question is, "Do you desire such a relationship with the Father?" I believe that you do, that you are convinced deep within that there is more than you are presently experiencing. It is my intention to help you move forward toward His embrace, and what follows will help you make that journey.

Granted, growing in the Lord's love and presence is not an uncostly or effortless pursuit. Like any relationship you must invest deeply, all the while trusting in the Lord's grace to give you the gift of His presence that could never be earned or deserved. But if you seek wholeheartedly He will be found (1 Chronicles 28:9). And saints of the past assure you that intimacy with the Lord touches all that it means to be human, mentally, emotionally, physically and spiritually. Men and women, like you, who have opened to that promise have experienced a transformation that almost betrays definition.

Intimacy With God Is For You

Jeanne Guyon lived and died in seventeenth century France, but her writings have profoundly affected Christians for over three hundred years. Concerned that the religious establishment of her day was politically driven yet powerless in spirit, Guyon wrote to affect change in the common person's experience of God. Prioritizing the interior life of intimacy and devotion with Christ, Madame Guyon inspired people to believe that God wanted a deep, personal relationship with all of His children. Though imprisoned in the Bastille for her beliefs, Guyon encouraged people to pursue God's embrace above all else, not only in her generation, but in every age since. Her writings have impacted such people as Fenelon, Zinzindorf, Wesley, Watchman Nee, Hudson Taylor and countless others.

In the introduction to the classic, *Experiencing the Depths of Jesus Christ*, Guyon writes:

> ...if you will take the trouble to seek God in your own heart, and if you sincerely forsake your sins so that you may draw near to Him, you shall find Him.

33

Some of you may doubt that God can actually be found so easily. If so, do not merely take my word for it. Try for yourself what I an proposing to you. For I am sure that your own experience will convince you that the reality is far greater than what I have told you.[2]

Madame Guyon's encouragement to launch out in pursuit of God moved thousands, even tens of thousands, to begin the journey to God's embrace. What resulted is part of the record of church history. Men and women ignited with a passionate love for God birthed churches, denominations, missionary movements and evangelistic campaigns as the fruit of their new relationship with Him. Intimacy with God became a reality for people who, like so many today, thought such an experience was not possible, at least not for them.

A.W. Tozer, known as the prophet of the twentieth century, wanted to stir the modern Christian man and woman to know God more deeply. Undoubtedly influenced by the writings of Guyon, Tozer believed that experiencing God's real presence was the privilege and promise of every believer. A prolific writer, Tozer is best known for his volume titled, *The Pursuit of God*. He felt that modern evangelical scholarship lacked the fire of God's presence. As a result people were missing what they needed most. Tozer wrote,

> For it is not mere words that nourish the soul, but God Himself, and unless and until the hearers find God in personal experience they are not the better for having heard the truth. The Bible is not an end in itself, but a means to bring men to an intimate and satisfying knowledge of God, that they may enter into Him, that they may delight in His presence, may taste and know the inner sweetness of the very God Himself in the core and center of their hearts.[3]

A.W. Tozer continues in *The Pursuit of God* to show the reader a pathway to intimacy. He encourages people to seek

God as the very Treasure of life, for, as Tozer puts it, "The person who has God has all things in one."[4]

Guyon and Tozer each reinforce the truth that experiencing the intimate presence of God is for all of us. You and I were made to daily journey to His embrace and will never be satisfied until we do. All other pursuits and passions will ultimately disappoint and fall far short of our needs. Only God will fill the hunger that gnaws away deep within us all. And praise His name, He anxiously and affectionately waits to satisfy the longing of each and every seeking heart.

The Bible Tells You So!

Certainly the testimony of scripture bears witness to the fact that seeking intimacy with God is to be your first and foremost concern. Look at the teaching of Jesus Himself. Over and over again the Lord called His followers to draw close to Him in meaningful fellowship. Consider the incident that took place in the home of the Lord's friend Lazarus, recorded in Luke 10. Jesus and His disciples went traveling through the village of Bethany and decided to stop and spend time with Lazarus, Martha and Mary.

Scripture tells us that the two sisters chose completely different responses to Christ's presence that day. Mary sat at his feet, listening to every word Jesus spoke. Martha was distracted, busy at work in the kitchen preparing a meal for her guests. Resentful of Mary's "laziness," Martha tried to enlist Jesus for what she believed to be a much needed rebuke of Mary. Instead, our Lord applauded Mary's response, telling Martha that her sister was investing in something far more important than service. Mary chose to prioritize relationship, which Jesus said could never be taken away from her. Jesus was not choosing one sister over the other. He was calling both to prioritize intimacy with Him above all else.

More than once I have listened as people present the case for an unhealthy dichotomy between service and the pursuit of intimacy. It is as if there is a free choice to be made between two equal yet very different investments. And most Christians, particularly those in evangelical churches, seem to be encouraged to choose activity over contemplation. But as author Frank Tuoti reminds us, this is most certainly not the lesson for us from the story of Mary and Martha. He writes:

> St. Bernard (of Clairvaux) reminds us that Martha and Mary are "sisters" and should not be separated. Our Lord's rebuke of Martha hinges not on the fact that she was sweating over a hot stove, but that she did not take time from her chores to contemplate Truth which was right in front of her. We, who are tempted to seek activity as an escape from prayer and periods of solitude, need to be mindful that not only is Truth right in front of us, but intimately within us, awaiting our undivided attention. The refusal of those engaged in the active life to set aside time for prayer, to contemplate Truth, makes for a mediocre and joyless life-a life that soon becomes bothersome, wearisome, and personally unrewarding. However, the contemplative who does not eventually reach out to others in compassionate service faces an even more foreboding fate.[5]

In the Sermon on the Mount, recorded in Matthew, Jesus stuns His listeners with these words. "Not everyone who says to me Lord, Lord will enter the Kingdom of Heaven." Jesus told His followers that neither miracles, prophesy nor power over demons was central to Kingdom life. Many, according to Christ, will have performed such service, yet ultimately hear Jesus say, "I never knew you, away from me"(Matthew 7:21-23).

These words, like few others in scripture, show how important it is that you have a dynamic relationship with Christ Jesus. Knowing Him stands above and precedes all else, even sacrificial service and astounding displays of miraculous power. Jesus came to earth to demonstrate God's passionate love for you and to provide a means by which you could be reunited with the Father. Do you realize how deeply God loves you? Have you considered the lengths to which He has gone to draw you into His embrace? Would He go to the cross and then not provide a path to that intimate embrace? Author Brennan Manning believes that, unfortunately, many Christians do not grasp the reality of God's unshakable love. He writes:

> Many Christians have never grabbed aholt of God. They do not know, really know, that God dearly and passionately loves them. Many accept it theoretically; others in a shadowy sort of way. While their belief system is invulnerable, their faith in God's love for them is remote and abstract. They would be hard-pressed to say that the essence of their faith commitment is a love affair between God and themselves. Not just a *simple* love affair, but a *furious* love affair.[6]

I want you to consider the biblical metaphor for the church, "bride of Christ." Can there be any question but that relationship is of primary importance? Who would want a marriage based on service rather than intimacy? While a husband and wife may do things for each other, such acts are not what gives their marriage meaning. It is relationship and intimacy that defines being together. Love, affection and commitment are the heart of marriage, flowing out into acts of service and devotion. I know of not one marriage based on love that does not translate into deeds. But I know of countless couples who do for each other but have no loving relationship. For Jesus and His bride, intimacy is to be first and foremost. It is to be a marriage of passionate love that overflows into selfless acts of devotion and delight. Jesus intends for you to be such a bride and He is most certainly that kind of husband, beckoning you to press into intimacy with Him. Your relationship with Christ is to be nothing short of breathtaking! Passionate! Exciting! Jesus loves you and wants to have you nestled in His arms of love. Can you even imagine the wonder and delight of such an intimate moment with Him? It is for you!

Recently, I was taken aback by the words of Christ recorded in John 10:14, 15. Jesus said, "I am the Good Shepherd. I know My sheep and My sheep know me, just as the Father knows Me and I know the Father, and I lay down My life for the sheep." Notice that Jesus compares your relationship with Him to His relationship with the Father. He is telling you that you, His sheep, can know God, not simply with a cognitive understanding, but in intimate fellowship and unity, similar to His relationship to the Father. By looking to Jesus you will see the quality of relationship with the Heavenly Father that is available to you. God loves you and wants to be ever close and very, very real. Granted, it is a journey, but all along the path the fruit of His love grows, there for your nourishment and delight. Brennan Manning describes that relationship in his book, *The Signature of Jesus.*

> Jesus lived for God. The central theme in the personal life of Jesus of Nazareth was his growing intimacy with, trust in, and love for his Father. His innerlife was centered on God. For him the Father meant everything, "Father , glorify your son that your son might glorify you." The will of the Father was the air he breathed. "I do nothing on my own, but only what I see the Father doing." The Father's will was a river of life, a bloodstream from which he drew life more profoundly than from his mother. "Whoever does the will of my Father is my mother, my brother, and my sister." He lived secure in his Father's acceptance. "As the Father has loved me, so have I loved you."[7]

The testimony and teaching of Jesus points to this one truth: You can grow to experience the presence and fellowship of the Lord, not just in heaven, but here on earth. It is His gift to you, received when you commit to this impassioned pursuit. Think of what this means. Christianity will not simply be a set of beliefs, but a relationship with the Lord that is, at times, genuinely present and experienced in your spirit. There is living water for you to drink.

The Apostle Paul prioritized relationship with the Lord in his own life. Nowhere is this made clearer than in his letter to the church in Philippi. He wrote:

> *What is more, I consider everything a loss compared to the surpassing greatness of knowing Christ Jesus my Lord, for whose sake I have lost all things. I consider them rubbish, that I may gain Christ and be found in Him.* — Philippians 3:8, 9

Paul believed and taught that knowing the Lord is life's purpose. All else is second at best, even rubbish when compared with gaining Christ! Intimacy with Jesus, according to Paul, is the greatest single goal of your life. He believed that knowing Christ is the joy of the Christian experience.

Sometimes it seems that we Christians major in what Christ does for us, grossly under-emphasizing the call to relationship. The benefits of salvation, provision, healing, spiritual gifts and the like are for many believers the focus of attention. But it is the Person behind these blessings that is central to faith. He is the Treasure, the Pearl of great price, the Gift of the Father to you, His beloved Child. As such, you should seek Him above all else, even above the blessings of faith.

Peter taught that grace, abundance and, in fact, all you need for life and godliness come through your knowledge of Jesus. He wrote,

> *Grace and peace be yours in abundance through the knowledge of God and of Jesus our Lord. His divine power has given us everything we need for life and godliness through our knowledge of Him....* — 2 Peter 1:2, 3

Can there be any doubt but that you are called to grow in relationship with the Lord? Scripture is so clear on this point. The Christian life is about intimacy with God, through Christ Jesus. To prioritize anything else is to miss the very heart of God's redemptive plan. And unfortunately, many do miss this blessing, assuming that this type of experience with Christ is for the limited few. Not so!

In his letter to the Ephesian church, Paul revealed his heart passion for Jesus and his concern that all believers develop a relationship with Him. These words, penned by Paul himself, have come to represent for me the first steps to such intimacy. He wrote: "I keep asking that the God of our Lord Jesus Christ, the glorious Father, may give you the Spirit of wisdom and revelation so that you may know Him better" (Ephesians 1:17).

Where does such a relationship begin? I believe Scripture teaches you that it all starts by asking. You must simply tell God that it is your desire to journey to His embrace, requesting that He unleash the Spirit of wisdom and revelation upon you to serve this critical pursuit. And the promise of Scripture is that if you ask in faith, God will respond. Do you hear that? He will respond!

Seeking The Kingdom First

Before concluding this chapter, I want to go back to my encounter with Scott. Because of some significant tensions in his ministry, Scott began meeting with me for help. In part he came because he knew my background in church growth and administration. Scott felt over his head in his responsibilities and was desperate for advice.

His list of concerns was long and legitimate, focusing on skill development as pastor for Christian education. I did give Scott guidance on ministry issues, but my primary concern was his relationship with the Lord. Each week I challenged him to press into God more, suggesting specific ways to encounter His presence. Initially, it was clear from Scott's response that service was his greatest concern, not devotion. Even though we had addressed various issues related to his job over a several-week period, Scott's frustration level was still quite high.

Convinced that his priorities were misplaced, I finally asked Scott permission for a one-week experiment. I wanted to control his schedule for seven days, setting aside all other concerns to focus on his time before the Lord. It took a bit of convincing, but Scott agreed. I immediately slotted in two hours a day for spiritual disciplines that would open the way to intimacy. I also asked Scott to call me at the end of each day to discuss what was or was not happening. At the end of one week I promised to back off my insistence regarding relationship and serve Scott as he desired. What happened was truly exciting, best described in Scott's own words:

> "Dear Terry,
> It was only a few short months ago that I told you I did not believe an intimate relationship with the Lord was for me. You helped me see that it was not only possible, but essential. In recent weeks this has all become so very real to me. God's presence in my life has become a source of strength and direction during a very difficult time. As you suggested, I have allowed the pain to drive me into His arms. There, God has challenged every idol I have turned to before Him. Most of all, He has shown me my own rebellion. By the strength of His love, I have learned to repent and let go of everything but Him. Every day I now meet with Him, and I can honestly say I am finding greater and greater freedom. Thanks.
> Lovingly,
> Your Brother Scott"

The priority of the Christian life has been clearly established. You are invited to enter into a life-changing relationship with God. This relationship is with a living Person who longs to be with you, to love you, and to experience your life. Granted, such a pursuit is not without its barriers and costs. Yet, the surpassing greatness of His presence makes the investment worth it all. The following prayer, written by Stephen Brown, may be a good place for you to start. Would you pray this right now?

> Father, I want to know you. I want to speak from the depth of my experience of you, not my knowledge about you. I want our relationship to be more than a formal relationship. I desire intimacy with you more than anything else. I ask that, whatever it takes, you would reveal yourself to me and that you would allow me to be close to you and to trust you more than I trust a doctrine or a religious formula.[8]

Questions For Discussion And Review

1. Can you identify with Scott? What have been your feelings about developing an intimate walk with God?

2. Have you ever launched out to have a devotional life, only to get frustrated and fail? Why?

3. What did A.W. Tozer mean when he said, "The Bible is not an end in itself"? What is the ultimate purpose of God's word?

4. Read Luke 10:38-42. Who do you most identify with in this story and why? What did Jesus mean when He said that Mary chose that which would last forever?

5. Which choice are you making?

6. What did Jesus mean in Matthew 7:21-23 when He said, "I never knew you, away from me"?

7. Read Philippians 3:8,9. How important was knowing Christ to Paul? How important is it to you?

8. Read Stephen Brown's prayer once again. Does this represent your heart? If so, bow and tell the Lord about it right now.

Chapter Three

Allowing God
To Draw You Into Intimacy

By age 45, Frank Laubach would have been commended for living a productive and sacrificial life in service to the Lord. That is, by everyone except Frank Laubach himself. While in the Philippines as a missionary in the 1930's, he concluded that there must be more to following after God than he was presently experiencing. Lonely and far from home, he embarked on what he called "an experiment" to become increasingly aware of the vibrant presence of God in his life.

Convinced that Jesus lived each moment full of His Father's presence, Frank Laubach prayed to live the rest of his days attentive to the will and wonder of God. For the next forty years he prioritized abiding in the presence of God above all else. Out of that experience Laubach wrote extensively, seeking to lead others in what he believed to be the privilege of the Christian experience. Growing ever close to God, and experiencing His real touch was, for Laubach, the ultimate joy of faith. Frank Laubach believed that such a relationship was there for anybody. He wrote:

> The notion that religion is dull, stupid and sleepy is abhorrent to God ... If you are weary of some sleepy form of devotion, probably God is as weary

of it as you are. Shake out of it, and approach Him in one of the countless fresh directions.

Humble folk often believe that walking with God is above their heads, or that they may "lose a good time," if they share all their joys with Christ. What a tragic misunderstanding to regard Him as a killer of happiness! A chorus of joyous voices round the world fairly sing that spending their hours with the Lord is the most thrilling joy ever known, and that beside it a ball game or a horse race is stupid. Spending time with the Lord is not a grim duty. And if you should forget Him for minutes or even days, do not groan or repent, but begin anew with a smile. Every moment can be a fresh beginning.[9]

Regardless of the present state of your Christian life, a fresh beginning awaits you. You can move forward toward a richer relationship with the Lord, and as with all things it begins with the first step: Asking the Lord to birth this hunger for intimacy deep within your heart. In this chapter we will be taking a look at God's part in drawing you into such a relationship. In the following chapters the discussion will focus on what you need to do along the journey to His embrace.

Pursuing Intimacy With God Is A Process

There are several very important things you must understand about devoting time to pursuing God. First, growing in a deep relationship with the Lord is a continual process. It is not so much a destination as it is a journey. Imagine that out before you is an expansive horizon. You fix your eyes on some majestic point in the distance and begin to walk toward it. As you move closer to the chosen point on the horizon, an amazing thing happens. What was once far away is now close at hand. Yet an entirely new and previously unseen horizon looms before you. The horizon itself is never reached, for there is always more to behold out in the distance.

So it is with pursuing the Lord. By the power of the Holy Spirit, you can move to a new level of understanding and intimacy with God. It will be exciting, rewarding and awe-inspiring, even beyond expectation. The potential of this anticipated closeness will make you think, "If only I could get to this point in my walk with the Lord I will have arrived. It is what I have always longed for and what will ultimately satisfy my spiritual hunger." Yet once there with God, an entirely new potential for an even deeper relationship can be seen in the horizon, beckoning you on to new vistas with Him. No matter where you are in Christ, there is always more, much more. More than you could even dream about or imagine.

You will find that you never feel as though you have arrived, but instead will be continually "arriving" in His embrace. As long as you move toward the Lord you will grow in spiritual health and well-being. There will still be peaks and valleys on the journey, but you will find the Lord Himself is at each point along the way, revealing Himself and gracing more and more of His presence in your life. What you experience of Him will only inspire you to press on for even more of the priceless Treasure that is Himself.

God's Part In Your Journey To His Embrace

What exactly is God's part in your developing an ever-deepening intimacy with Him? In simplest terms, it is God who initiates and enables any level of relationship you might have with Him. You must never forget that you are, apart from His grace, a weak and sinful human being destined for an eternity separated from all that is good. No effort on your part could ever span that chasm, regardless of how bright, noble or costly it may have been. Motivated by unfathomable love, God sent Jesus to die for your sin, cleanse you of unrighteousness and reconcile you with Himself. Through Christ you have been adopted as His children, and made an

47

heir of indescribable Kingdom blessings, not the least of which is an ever-deepening relationship with Him.

Redemption and all its benefits are totally a gift of His grace. As God pours out the living water of His favor, you position yourself in its flow, receive His glorious refreshing and then respond by living a life that glorifies Him. And in truth, even that level of your response is a work of His grace since it is His Spirit that enables you to walk in faith and obedience.

And so, in pursuing intimacy with God, you must begin by recognizing that it is His love that has made such a relationship even possible. It is not your desire but His that has birthed the potential of abiding in His majestic presence. As you move forward in divine pursuit, it is important to confess humbly that every step forward, from initial desire to moments in ecstatic union is thoroughly dependent on Him. It is His grace, not your work, that makes the pilgrimage possible.

One of my favorite passages of Scripture is found in the book of Ezekiel. It portrays God as a faithful and generous Shepherd who goes to great lengths to care for the sheep He loves. The passage is filled with "I will" statements that are listed below. They clearly show that moving toward wholeness and well-being is dependent on His grace.

I will search for my sheep;
I will look for them;
I will rescue them;
I will bring them out from the nations;
I will bring them out from their own land;
I will pasture them;
I will tend them;
I will search for the lost;
I will bring back strays;
I will bind up the injured;
I will save my flock;
I will place over them one shepherd, my servant David;
I will make a covenant of peace;

I will bless them;
I will multiply the number of people;
I will increase the number of men and animals;
I will make you prosper;
I will sprinkle clean water on you;
I will cleanse you;
I will give you a new heart;
I will put my Spirit in you.[10]

Reading this list of God-initiated and God-sustained blessings should birth within your heart incredible humility, thanks, devotion and hope. Growing close to Him is not an impossible burden dependent solely on your own effort. It is a potential reality for you because He has made it so. You need to move forward in faith, trusting that God will, through Christ, draw you into the arms of His intimate embrace. Whenever you are weak or weary or wondering if you will ever grow beyond your present relationship with Christ, read these promises. Invariably the Holy Spirit will breathe life into your soul, assuring you that the journey toward intimacy is not dependent on your efforts. God has already acted and promises to care for you continually. You need only respond in faith and obedience.

God Works To Prepare You For Intimacy

I am sure you know Romans 8:28 and find hope in God's promise to work through "all things" to benefit your life. However, the next verse is critical to understanding why He does this. Paul wrote:

> And we know that in all things God works for the good of those who love Him, who have been called according to His purpose. For those God foreknew He also predestined to be conformed to the image of His Son....
> — Romans 8:28, 29

The Father is working through the "all things" of life to make you more like Jesus. This process is essential to pursuing the type of intimacy with God that Jesus modeled while on earth. Yes, it is true that at new birth you are positionally sanctified and reckoned as righteous before God. But practically, you must continually surrender to His ongoing work in your life, day by day, issue upon issue.

It is the Holy Spirit who actively works to conform you to the image of Christ Jesus. He is involved at every point along the way in your spiritual development. Nothing significant occurs in your spiritual walk apart from Him. You must come to understand, appreciate and submit to the Spirit's ministry. You need to recognize His presence deep within and regularly fellowship with Him.

It is not my purpose here to develop a thorough treatment on the Holy Spirit. I refer you to either *Surprised by the Holy Spirit*, by Jack Deere or *The Holy Spirit*, by Billy Graham. But I do want to leave little doubt in the importance of His role in God's work of drawing you increasingly to Himself. It is the Spirit, God's *Flame of Love* as Saint John of the Cross called Him, that works to bring you ever close to the all-consuming love of the Father above.

Purging And Perfecting

It may be helpful to divide the work God does through the Holy Spirit into two categories. In preparing you for increasing intimacy, He moves in your life to purge and perfect you. In purging, God seeks to excise from your life all that is not of Him whether it be the sins that enslave, the wounds that paralyze or the levels of demonization that oppress. God the Holy Spirit makes a way of cleansing, healing and freedom. He does this over time, given your willing submission to His sanctifying activity. Granted, it is a lifelong process, yet each time you surrender to this work, you draw ever nearer to the intimacy you desire.

Simultaneously, God increasingly fills your life with qualities of the Kingdom. It is a perfecting process, a passing from the life of the flesh to the life and empowerment of the Holy Spirit. As you die to the works of the flesh there is increasing room for the flow of righteousness, peace and joy. This includes nurturing the fruits, gifts and empowerment of the Spirit in your life as well as everything it means to be clothed in Christ's love, mind and strength. This is all possible through the sacrifice Jesus made for you at Calvary. This purging and perfecting brings your life into the harmony with God so necessary to intimacy. There is no way to move forward toward His embrace apart from this two-fold work. Death to self and life to the Spirit does not come to you easily. There is certain cost and, at times, some pain. Yet, the rewards of God's presence and reality of His nearness go far beyond even your most generous expectation. The delight and, at times, ecstasy of His embrace make even the greatest sacrifice along the way pale in comparison. They are, as Paul said, light and momentary—not worth considering in light of the surpassing glory of knowing Him! (Romans 8:18).

Anticipating The Process Of Developing Intimacy With God

It is impossible to predict precisely what the process of purging and perfecting will be like. Each pilgrimage is shaped by God to fit uniquely the work that needs to be accomplished in each individual. Yet there are, I believe, seasons of cleansing and growth that are more often than not experienced by most all who pursue a deepening relationship with the Lord. Anticipating and understanding the shape and purpose of these stages of development will help you reap the change and blessing found in each. During such times God will be revealing the sins, wounds and lies that create disharmony in your life and keep you from experiencing His presence. Perceiving His work and responding in faith and obedience are essential to your spiritual growth and personal well-being. Every season of life is shaped by God for that very purpose.

One of the most important lessons I learned in my own ongoing pilgrimage toward intimacy with the Lord has come from the writings of an eighteenth century French mystic. Jean-Pierre de Caussade served as the spiritual director for the Visitation nuns in northeast France. His teachings were written down by the nuns and preserved unpublished for decades. Today his insights on the spiritual life are found in a book titled *The Sacrament Of The Present Moment*.

Jean-Pierre de Caussade's most valuable contribution to spiritual formation relates directly to anticipating the work of God during the changing phases of your pilgrimage toward intimacy. Most of us fight against the difficult and trying moments that come in life. De Caussade encouraged believers of his day to find God in everything and anything that life brought their way, whether easy or hard, light or heavy. He taught from his own experience, encouraging his hearers to listen for the voice of God present in every moment and circumstance. He said,

> You are seeking God, dear sisters, and He is everywhere. Everything proclaims Him to you, everything reveals Him to you, everything brings Him to you. He is by your side, over you, around and in you. Here is His dwelling and yet you still seek Him. Ah! You are searching for God, the idea of God in His essential being. You seek perfection and it lies in everything that happens to you—your suffering, your actions, your impulses are the mysteries under which God reveals Himself to you.[11]

To de Caussade, each moment is a revelation of God, allowed by Him to fulfill His purpose in people's lives. All is an instrument of sanctification which ultimately serves to bring His children into conformity with Christ. Trusting His inherent goodness regardless of what comes your way will enable you to lay hold of God's intended blessing. "It is the will of God that gives everything, whatever it may be, the power to form Jesus Christ in the center of our being. This will knows no limits."[12]

Embracing this understanding of life's circumstances will position you to cooperate with God's work. The reward becomes yours by anticipating and surrendering to the lesson of "the present moment." Rather than praying, "God change my situation," you can cry out, "God, show me Yourself in this circumstance. I offer this moment to You as a way of shaping and changing me. May I surrender to Your work so that it may bring me into ever-increasing harmony with You." Granted, this concept does not fit with popular Christian philosophies that prioritize "name it and claim it" solutions to life's problems. Instead, you will be challenged to find something in life more important than escaping pain and discomfort. You will be discovering God in the midst of difficulty and trial, and growing to love and trust him more and more.

Changing Seasons That Will Transform You

There are, as I have already stated, various and very different seasons that God may use in your pilgrimage toward intimacy. What follows is a brief discussion of four of these, which I believe are common to spiritual development. I am not saying that you will experience each of these seasons, nor that they come only once or in any predictable order. I am simply identifying what has been consistently used by God throughout history to draw men and women more deeply into His embrace. Each comes when and as often as God chooses to use it in your cleansing and growth. He sovereignly designs the times, it is yours but to respond in faith and obedience. My hope is that this discussion will better prepare you to reap the fruit God intends.

Seasons of Sweet Embrace

In January of 1992, I was reading Psalm 20 and was deeply moved by verse four. It reads, "May He give you your heart's desire." I felt the Holy Spirit quickening within me, beckoning me to lay before God my deepest request. For some time He had been igniting within me an ever-increasing passion to know Him more. Worn out by the mismanagement of ministry demands, I wanted to draw closer to God in devotion and love. And so I prayed for a more intimate relationship with Him, marking the date in my Bible as a memorial of remembrance.

Within a few weeks the door opened for me to take a three-month sabbatical from my responsibilities at the church. This afforded me the privilege of spending long periods in prayer, reading and Scripture. Day by day the waters of refreshing poured across the parched ground of my soul. Within weeks I could sense an awakening of my spiritual senses. There was a sweetness and delight to those days as I had never known in the past. God was so close in prayer. Scripture came alive as I read, not giving information alone, but drawing me into His presence. This season came as a gift of God's grace, laying a foundation of intimacy upon which my future was to be built. While the dark night of the soul was yet ahead of me, these days initiated a hunger for more of the Lord that helped sustain me through the trials and difficulties yet to come.

This time was, in some ways, reminiscent of the narrative in the Song of Songs. The young girl has been overwhelmed by the presence of her lover. She declares,

> I delight to sit in his shade
> and his fruit is sweet to my taste.
> He has taken me to the banquet hall and his banner
> over me is love.
> Strengthen me with raisins, refresh me with apples,
> For I am faint with love.
> His left arm is under my head
> and his right arm embraces me.
> — Song of Solomon 2:3-6

Her words reveal an intoxication with the lover's presence and a contentment to rest there with him.

In the mid-seventies there was a small church in rural Pennsylvania where a revival took place among area young people. Several dozen teenagers came to confess Christ and were aflame with an obvious passion to know God more. For a lengthy season these youthful zealots were consumed with a most contagious love for the Lord. I remember being moved by their enthusiasm for Bible study, witnessing and most of all prayer meetings. There were times when these young believers spent entire nights in corporate prayer. And throughout this time the sweetness of the Lord's presence was most satisfying and enjoyable. It was a season of delight they likely will never forget.

Such a time in spiritual pilgrimage is very sweet, innocent, exciting and exhilarating. In many ways it could be compared to teenage "puppy love," that at the moment seems so complete, so deep, so permanent. In our immaturity we would stay there forever, content to rest in this level of relationship with God. For certainly it is new, alive and intoxicating. But by His grace God will not allow it.

Your Father knows that this is but the shallows, and far greater experiences of intimacy and harmony await you. But reaching those levels of oneness demand more difficult days, when His presence is not as sweet or obvious. These seasons are designed to purge you of selfish motivation, faithlessness and immaturity. They are meant to forge within your life a deeper hunger for true love and intimacy with God, enabling you to contain far more of His priceless Treasure. But here, where it all starts, God allows you that intoxicating first taste of His presence that prepares you to seek Him above all else life affords. Make no mistake, this experience of His presence is real, important and at some levels transforming. But by His grace He will position you to long for deeper and more consuming encounters of His love.

Seasons of Silence

Following the beloved's season of delight in her lover's arms comes a period of separation. Without warning, he is gone. Longing for his nearness, she sets out to find him, fired all the more by the memory of his embrace. The beloved goes looking for her betrothed.

All night long on my bed I looked for the one my heart loves!
I looked for him but did not find him.
I will get up now and go about the city, through its streets and squares;
I will search for the one my heart loves.
So I looked for him but did not find him.
The watchman found me as they made their rounds in the city.
Have you seen the one my heart loves?
— Song of Solomon 3:1, 2

There will be times when it seems as though God is gone, unresponsive to your pleas, His words of love silent. It may seen as though nothing is happening in your life, no movement in your pursuit of His embrace. Rather than feeling the closeness you so long for, you will sense that God is not there, not listening, not drawing you into His tender arms. In truth, a deep work is taking place in your spirit, all the while preparing you for even more of Him. He has withdrawn the sweetness of "first love" in order to move you to the depths of forever love.

Frankly, you may not always respond well to these days. Anxious by His apparent absence you may become nervous and introspective, asking, "What have I done? Where is the sin? What can I do to bring back the delight of His presence? Pray more? Repent more? Serve more? What is the key?" Certainly prayer, repentance and service are always to be part of your life. But nothing you do manipulates the moment. Such times have a purpose in God's plan and must run their course.

Richard Foster experienced such a season in his own spiritual pilgrimage. He wrote about it in *Prayer: Finding the Hearts True Home.*

Allow me to share with you one time when I entered the Prayer of the Forsaken. By every outward standard things were going well. Publishers wanted me to write for them. Speaking invitations were too numerous and too gracious. Yet through a series of events it seemed clear to me that God wanted me to retreat from public activity. In essence God was saying," Keep quiet!" and so I did. I stopped all public speaking, I stopped all writing, and I waited. At the time this began I did not know if I would ever speak or write again — I rather thought I would not. As it turned out, this fast from public life lasted about eighteen months.

I waited in silence. And God was silent too. I joined in the Psalmist's query: " How long will you hide your face from me?" (Psalm 13:1) The answer I got: nothing. Absolutely nothing! There were no sudden revelations. No penetrating insights. Not even gentle assurance. Nothing!… as best as I can discern, the silence of God month after month was a purifying silence.[13]

About such periods Madame Guyon wrote,

Now why would God do that? Dear saint of God you must learn the ways of your Lord. Yours is a God who hides Himself. He hides Himself for a purpose. Why? His purpose is to rouse you from spiritual laziness. His purpose in removing Himself from you is to cause you to pursue Him.[14]

She goes on to recommend the following response to such seasons:

Await the return of His presence with patient love.
Spend time faithfully in worship and silence.
Wait in a spirit of humility, with contentment and resignation.[15]

You may find help from the lessons of Habbakuk. During a time of silence he continued to lay his request before the Lord while staying faithful to stand his post as a watchman of Israel. God's silence did not lead him to run in panic, but instead to wait in faithful anticipation. (See Habbakuk 2:1) So must you respond in faith, continuing to come to Him in worship and devotion, trusting that in His appointed time God's goodness will again be experienced deep within your heart. Lay out your concern, even complaint, before Him, all the while trusting that He is deep within doing a work far beyond sense and comprehension. In the seasons of silence our Lord is still very active, shaping you for ever-increasing harmony and intimacy.

Seasons in the Desert

All Christians go through desert experiences. They are seasons of testing and character building foundational to spiritual growth. Nothing will help you understand the purpose and dynamic of such times better than the biblical narrative of Israel's journey from Egypt to Canaan. Following 400 years of bondage, God set his people free. Through the leadership of Moses, he placed them on a course to the promised land, by way of the savage wilderness. There, apart from the normal provisions of life, He would test and shape a people capable of living in Canaan as His holy and obedient nation. The desert brought with it hunger, thirst, enemy threat and devastating boredom. But it also was a season of incredible manifestation of the nearness and provision of God. If and when God's people responded in faith, the Lord Almighty proved His love and might. But incessant doubt, division and complaining extended their stay in the desert, bringing for many the tragic fate of never reaching His promised land.

Seasons in the desert will not be much different for you. They are times of dynamic tension between God's incredible nearness and the absence of so many of the comforts and provisions you normally take for granted. The purpose seems clear. It is a place of stripping away. All the things you count on for safety and security are less attainable. More often than not, they have become gods in your life. And these gods must be cast down and destroyed so that your trust in the living God can increase. As it does, the obstacles to intimacy fall increasingly away, opening wide before you

58

the promised land of His embrace. The desert is not an easy time. But it is the place where you learn better than anywhere else that God is mighty, able when necessary to provide water where a rock once stood.

He is so very near, beckoning you to trust Him to provide what you need, as you need, when you need. The desert is the place of His miraculous intervention into your daily life. Each obstacle, deadline and due date is an opportunity for your growth. If you stay your post in trust and obedience, a miracle occurs. When you panic and manipulate, the rock is struck, or an Ishmael is born.

God wants you to trust Him unconditionally. I know this is difficult for many and takes time and healing. Yet He longs for you to believe that He is faithful to every promise, ready and willing to act on your behalf. His purpose in the desert is to forge in you unmovable, unwavering faith and unquestioning obedience. Do not grumble, complain or run. Hold fast, for your time here will not last. But the lessons of these days will serve you well in the journey toward God that is ahead.

Psalm 106 offers great advice on how to respond to the desert. There are within the text thirteen identifiable principles that, when followed, will keep you from missing the purposes God intends for this difficult, yet transforming season. During desert times God's word instructs you to:

Believe His promises (vs. 12)
Sing His praise (vs. 12)
Remember what He has done for you in the past (vs. 13)
Seek His counsel (vs. 13)
Do not give in to sinful desires (vs. 14)
Do not envy others (vs. 16)
Do not turn to familiar idols (vs. 19)
Do not despise the place God has you in (vs. 24)
Do not grumble (vs. 25)
Obey the Lord (vs. 25)

Do not strike out in anger (vs. 33)
Cry out to God in humility (vs. 44)
Praise the Lord! (vs. 48)

Seasons Of Darkness

Admittedly, the most difficult period that may come in your spiritual development is what Saint John of the Cross called "the Dark Night of the Soul." It is a time characterized by varying levels of pain, oppression and loss. It may involve some degree of suffering, be that emotional, physical or spiritual. I do not believe that all Christians experience this time of difficulty and trial. But it seems to be a tool used by God in some, particularly those who long for ever-deepening harmony and oneness with the Father.

Few in our modern Western Christian society accept the idea that suffering is in God's plan for their lives. Yet the testimony of Scripture and church history is unquestionably clear on this point. God may allow seasons of darkness to enter your life as a means of developing you into His holy and obedient children.

Countless Christians have written of the dark night through the centuries. Few have described it as well as Jean-Pierre de Caussade. He writes:

> There is a kind of saintliness when divine communication is precise and clear as daylight. But there is also a passive saintliness communicated by God through faith from the impenetrable darkness which surrounds his throne, in terms that are confused and obscure. Those who find this way are often afraid, like the prophet, to follow it and afraid of running into danger when walking through that darkness. Have no fear, faithful souls! That is where your path lies, the way along which God is guiding you. There is nothing safer or more sure than the dark night of faith. Follow anyway when faith is so obscure and darkness obliterates everything and the path can no longer be discerned.[16]

The question that immediately comes to mind is, "Why would God allow such a time to enter the lives of the children He loves?" The broad answer is to give you treasures you could never receive if you only lived a life of ease and abundance. There are things you will see and understand in the dark that are totally oblivious to you in the light. Also, there is often a necessary purging of impure motives that takes place, as well as a preparation for a new level of ministry.

The dark night of the soul can be painful and debilitating. Yet this time of brokenness can also become the source of incredible change and blessings. During the season of difficulty and oppression, God often reveals several impure motives and character sins that greatly affect your relationship with Him. God will possibly point out such sins as pride, anger and a preoccupation with importance. He will also expose weak places in the foundation of your faith that desperately need addressing. This season of weakness and suffering will shape an entirely new approach to ministry. Instead of moving toward service confident of your own abilities, you will come as wounded healer totally dependent on His strength. All of this will open the way for a new experience of God's love and nearness that you never knew before.

The Psalmist blessed the Lord for the time of affliction, saying that it put him back on course with God (Psalm 119:67, 75). Paul declared that a dark time in his own life birthed a greater dependence on the Lord (2 Corinthians 1:9). He taught the early Christians that suffering produced the necessary qualities of Christ in their lives (Romans 5:1-5). And James, the brother of our Lord went so far as to tell people to rejoice in trial, because the outcomes were priceless to their strength (James 1:2-4). These are but a few of the countless texts which teach you that God at times allows pain and suffering as a means of transforming your life.[17]

Saint John of the Cross, a sixteenth century Spanish mystic, wrote extensively on this subject in *Dark Night of the Soul*.

He concluded that there were several reasons why God allows suffering, including to:

Forge humility
Put people in touch with their inherent weakness
Exalt God's greatness
Break pride
Purify the soul
Set people free from spiritual laziness
Teach deeper spiritual truths
Help people pursue God rather than the things of God.

Saint John of the Cross believed that the final outcome of this work was a new harmony and oneness between the pilgrim and God.[18]

Of the "dark night" Foster writes:

> Through all of this, paradoxically, God is purifying our faith by threatening to destroy it. We are led to profound and holy distrust of all superficial drives and human strivings. We know more deeply than ever our capacity for infinite self deception. Slowly we are being taken off of vain securities and false allegiances. Our trust in all exterior and interior results is being shattered so that we can learn faith in God alone. Through our barrenness of soul God is producing detachment, humility, patience, perseverance.[19]

Your first reaction to seasons of darkness will probably include crying, "Get me out of here!" No one relishes pain, and your natural desire is to find a way of escape. But through the Holy Spirit's guidance, you will see that your first response should be to offer that difficulty to God. He can and will use it to conform you ever closer to Christ and draw you to Himself. The pain of this season is not that which harms. It is instead what Henri Nouwen called "labor pain" that precedes the birth of something good and exciting.[20]

As with each season discussed in this chapter, you must learn to find God there and submit to His revelation and restoration. Be assured, such a response is not always easy. But through the Holy Spirit's help you can pass through the dark cloud and bring out the Treasures hidden in those secret places. You can, through Him, find a peace far below the storm that births hope and promise for a new and exciting relationship with your Heavenly Father.

The seasons of purging and perfecting only last as long as they best serve your pursuit of God. On the other side of these times will be a richer, more fulfilling and a far deeper walk with Him. After passing through, the memory of the pain will grow dim, yet the intensity of His presence will grow greater. Like others you will even turn and bless what you once desired to escape. For the experience of His love and nearness is forever and in all ways worth it all.

Questions For Discussion And Review

1. What is meant by the statement, "Growing in intimacy with God is not so much a destination as it is a journey"?

2. What was meant by the statement that God initiates our pursuit of relationship with Him?

3. Why is the potential of relationship with God considered an act of grace?

4. Re-read the "I will" list found in this chapter. What happens to you as you read it? What does this tell you about God's activity in your life?

5. What does Romans 8:28 and 29 have to do with pursuing God's embrace?

6. Why is it important that we be sensitive to the Holy Spirit in our lives?

7. How does purging and perfecting relate to the pursuit of intimacy with God? Define each.

8. How do the following seasons serve the process of purging and perfecting?

Seasons of Sweet Embrace?

Seasons of Silence?

Seasons in the Desert?

Seasons of Darkness?

9. Which of these seasons have you experienced before and how did it affect your relationship with God?

Chapter Four

Positioning Yourself To Pursue Intimacy

Some years ago I had the privilege of sailing out of San Diego Bay with my good friend John Smith. (No kidding, that is really his name.) It was a fantastic day in mid-January, warm and sunny with a gray whale migration taking place right before our eyes. At the time, we were both pastoring in Pennsylvania where on that particular day it was -10 degrees and snowing. I remember well, because I called my wife to tell her about my wonderful adventure. She told me of shoveling our driveway in my absence!

What impressed me most that day was the power of the wind. As the sail was set the boat moved so gracefully across the water. The captain used the rudder to direct us along the coast to Tijuana, where off in the distance I could see an arena where bull fights were held. It was a most memorable day.

Yet, what if there had been no wind that day? Even with fine sails on a sleek vessel and an able seaman at the helm, we would have gone nowhere without the ocean breeze. All the right equipment and experience would have been useless. John and I could have repeatedly emptied our lungs blowing toward the sail. But in the end we would have still been dead in the water, going nowhere fast. It is the wind that made our journey along the coast the exciting and memorable trip it was.

In this chapter I want to discuss practical steps that position you to journey toward God's embrace. But from the very beginning let it be clear that apart from the empowerment of the Holy Spirit, these steps are impotent to bring lasting change in your life. Human effort alone is powerless to enhance intimacy with the Lord. It takes the constant activity of God as He chooses to breathe life upon the disciplines and efforts you offer.

Far too many people make the mistake of thinking that they can grow in the Lord if only they do the right things. They think that if they pray, read, study Scripture, fast and serve enough they will come to know God better. This approach to spiritual formation prioritizes performance as the key to Christian health and maturity. But it is a misunderstanding that is works-oriented, ultimately leading to frustration, burnout or lifeless discipleship.

The key to experiencing God's embrace is found in submitting to His activity. Practical disciplines of devotional life serve as sails. You must set them in anticipation of the Wind of His Spirit. Having plotted a course toward relationship with Him, you then raise the canvas of practical spiritual disciplines by faith. What you find is that God sovereignly determines when to empower your efforts and to what degree. You can never force His hand or manipulate His power to your own design and desire. Yours is but daily and faithfully to set sail with expectation and hope. Some days you will catch the wind in the sail of prayer, on others through worship or some different activity of devotion. You never know where or to what degree He will move. And sometimes all will be motionless and still. But each day if you are hungry to move closer to the Lord, spend quality time in intimate devotion, preparing to catch the wind.

Commitments That Position You To Pursue God's Embrace

There are, as already stated, forces that work directly against your pursuit of intimacy with God. Whether from the enemy, society or even at times from within yourself, these obstacles are not easily overcome. You must take radical steps to move against this heavy current of opposition, setting your course intentionally and intensively toward the Father's embrace.

While it is God's sovereign activity that enables this pursuit, you would do well to do your part. Using once again sailing as a metaphor, you must position the vessel of your life toward relationship with God, and set the sails that best catch the wind of His Spirit. These two categories of activity will be the focus of this and the next chapter. Here, I will discuss several practical principles that position you for the journey toward intimacy. Like a rudder, they will help keep you on the course you now most desperately desire. In the next chapter, I will highlight the disciplines of devotion that have been used biblically and historically as vehicles of God's empowerment. Remember that this journey demands your diligent and even sacrificial commitment. The steps that follow are to be embraced by prayerful determination and devotion, with the hope that God will move you ever close to His heart of love and delight.

Attentiveness

As a small boy I learned some invaluable lessons on awareness and attentiveness from my father. I mentioned in the introduction that I was raised in the fields and hills of western Pennsylvania, and that hunting was, for most young boys, a rite of passage. From early childhood, stories of hunting dogs, deer and small game abounded whenever and wherever uncles and cousins gathered. I listened with delight to each and every tale, always anticipating the day I would be old enough to go to the woods with them.

I learned quite young that the key to a successful trip was much more than knowing how to shoot a gun. It was far more important that I be attentive to the sights, sounds and signs of animals in the forest. A good hunter was ever aware of the tracks, movements and calls of nearby game. "Seeing" the evidence of deer or turkeys would make all the difference between success and failure.

I remember well my first deer hunt with my dad. A buck walked right by me, so close I could have touched it. But I didn't even see it. All the while, my dad watched from a distance, chuckling in realization that I had a lot more to learn before I would be reckoned a true hunter. I needed "eyes" to see and "ears" to recognize the abundance of wild life "hiding" all around me.

Our world is alive with the movement of God, yet most of us are tuned out. Possibly this verse from Elizabeth Barrett Browning's poem, "Aurora Leigh," says it best:

> *Earth's crammed with heaven,*
> *And every common bush afire with God;*
> *But only he who sees takes off his shoes;*
> *The rest sit round it and pluck blackberrys.*

For far too long I plucked berries from burning bushes, unaware of the presence of God in my midst. Expecting thunder and lightning-like encounters, I missed the whispers of His presence found in what had become for me the mundane in life. My "eyes" and "ears" were untrained and therefore insensitive to the sights and sounds of His glory all around. But, like a small boy learning the key to the woods, I am beginning to see movement, hear the sound of His coming and recognize His call off in the distance. And, again like a boy seeing his first deer, my heart beats with excitement, for I know he is coming ... hunting for me!

Whenever I have the opportunity, I recommend that people read Ken Gire's book, *Windows of the Soul*. Gire has learned to be attentive to God's presence in very human and earthy places. His writing serves as a textbook for every person wanting to enroll in a course of awareness. He argues that God shows up in the day-to-day events of our lives. Yet too many of us see only what is obvious to the senses, not God's activity behind every movement. Ken Gire instructs his readers in the importance of attentiveness and provides insight into "seeing" and "hearing" as never before. He writes,

> We reach for God in many ways. Through our sculptures and our scriptures. Through our pictures and our prayers. Through our writing and our worship. And through them He reaches for us.
>
> His search begins with something said. Ours begins with something heard. His begins with something shown. Ours, with something seen. Our search for God and His search for us meet at windows in our everyday experience. These are the windows of the soul.
>
> In a sense, it is something like spiritual disciplines for the spiritual undisciplined. In another sense, it is the most rigorous of the disciplines— the discipline of awareness. For we must always be looking and listening if we are to see the windows and hear what is being spoken to us through them.[21]

Kenneth Gire shows us that our encounters with people, our jobs, our world, our art, our dreams, our movies and our stories become unexpected parables through which God speaks. And every word beckons us to intimacy with Him.

The journey to God's embrace demands awareness and attentiveness. Without it you will possibly miss His voice that calls you to come closer still. He will speak to you through all that you offer Him, but will you hear ... will you see?

I believe the admonition of the Lord from Matthew chapter 26, verse 41, could serve well at this point; "Watch and pray." May you begin to look through the windows of life, hoping and longing to see God. And may you pray, asking the Lord to touch your eyes that you might behold His glory where before you only saw berries on a bush. At first it may be that you are not really confident of what you are actually seeing. But soon, very soon, by His grace you will see that your world is alive with God, "every bush ablaze." There you will fall and worship ... and by His grace feel his loving arms enfold you.

Time

One way that you position yourself to grow in the Lord is by investing time in the pursuit. And in our society finding a reserve of that precious resource is not always easy. Schedule demands seem to be increasing almost daily. In fact, for most of my friends, finding more time is becoming more important than earning more money! As Sir Walter Scott said, "Time is the stuff life is made of." Yet for most of us, the "stuffing" is being kicked out of our lives.

For the past several years I have had the opportunity to be more devoted to my relationship with the Lord. Where I previously set aside minutes, God has enabled me to give far more time. The benefits of this investment are almost unexplainable. Changes, exciting changes, have occurred in my relationship with God, my wife, my family, my ministry and my own emotional well-being. Jesus was not kidding when He commanded His followers to seek the Kingdom first, promising that all things would follow that priority (Matthew 6:33). It is true. An investment in intimacy with God reaps benefits in every area of a person's life.

Frankly, changing my priorities did not come by mere choice or act of the will. It was a necessity. After the dark and debilitating depression mentioned earlier, I lost all confidence in my personal gifts and abilities. This weakness forced me to spend extended seasons in prayer and Scripture reading each and every day. It was the only way I could move out to face the responsibilities that were before me.

But this problem became the doorway to a new and exciting walk with God. While at first I came before Him for strength, I soon became inebriated with the joy of just being in His presence. As a result, long after healing came to my emotions, the priority of spending time with Him has remained.

People often ask me, "How much time should I set aside for the disciplines of devotion?" Frankly, that varies from person to person. I do believe the greater the responsibilities of life, the more critical it is to give meaningful periods for the pursuit of God. The key is consistency and substance. Make sure your time before the Lord is regularly scheduled and long enough to impact your life substantially. Obviously, some people may not be led to spend as much time in devotion, while others even more. Begin where you can and make the time significant enough to make a difference.

Experience would lead me to suggest an approach to setting aside time with the Lord that is different from popular advice. Many Christian leaders recommend beginning with small "bites" of time and gradually increasing it over several months. The notion is that a little time will give birth to a lot of time. Frankly, I seldom see this translate into reality. Instead, I advise beginning with an initial larger block of time for a short season, and then moving to a more manageable amount as a consistent discipline.

For example, if it were your intention to spend thirty minutes a day in devotional disciplines, you should begin with one hour or more for two to three weeks. Knowing that this sacrifice is for a limited time enables you to embrace it willingly and enthusiastically. And this concentrated beginning will help firmly establish the devotional disciplines in your life. You would move to your daily thirty minute commitment from strength, not weakness. I have consistently seen this approach bear positive and lasting fruit in the lives of those who embraced it.

In *Let Prayer Change Your Life*, Becky Tirabassi made an interesting paraphrase of John 15. Everywhere Scripture used the phrase "abide" or "remain in me," she substituted "spend time with me." Doing this, she writes, will convince a person that setting aside time with the Lord is worth the investment. She wrote,

> "... you have the following reasons for having a regular daily appointment with God:
> If you spend time with God, He will spend time with you (v.4).
> You *cannot* bear fruit unless you spend time with God (v.4).
> But you will bear much fruit if you spend time with Him (v. 5).
> Anyone who does not spend time with God will be thrown away like a branch, picked up, thrown into the fire, and burned (v.6).
> If you spend time with Him and His words spend time in you, 'Ask whatever you wish, and it will be given to you'." (v.7)
> Now spend time basking in God's love (v.9)!
> It appears clear that Jesus wants us:
> To spend time with Him for the furtherance of His Kingdom.
> To be empowered to do His works.
> To know Him and His ways so intimately that whatever we ask will be given to us!
>
> Doesn't it work that way in your closest relationships? You know their personality, their preferences, and their precepts, and you rarely overstep, infringe, or misread them because you know a lot about them before you ask of them. That is the result of spending time with God as well![22]

Spending time with God positions you to know Him better. Life will get busy and forces will align against this commitment. But by His Spirit you can invest this resource of meaningful periods in His presence and be assured, the fruit will be rich and eternal.

Place

Eric has been my friend for over a decade. He is, without question, one of the most social people I have ever known. He loves to be around his friends. Somehow they seem to give life to Eric. They also have, at times, served to silence the real and important questions that are plaguing him deep inside.

In recent years I have watched Eric respond to the challenge of solitude. Previously, quiet time to him meant being alone with the Lord in a busy restaurant while reading his Bible. After I talked to Him about the need for true silence, he bought ear plugs for his regular visit to the diner! He told me this "really helped him hear from God." Finally Eric got the point and began to retreat to a quiet place where the noises and distractions of life were eliminated. And then and there, true movement began to occur in his ever-deepening relationship with the Lord.

You would do well to find the place, or places, that positively impact your pursuit of God. Your normal life is probably far too loud to consistently hear the whispers of your Lord. Sights and sounds have the potential of drowning out God's voice and your own inner voice, which is pleading for rest and quiet in His presence. Whether it is a special room, a spot in a local park, or a hideaway in the woods, "place" makes a difference.

As the Lord quickened my heart to pursue intimacy, finding the right place became a priority. Initially, I built a small room in my garage, equipping it with only those things that would enhance seeking Him. I also located a few special spots outside that would allow for some variety. But in each location, silence was critical. I needed to be alone with God, without the visitation of distracting noise or curious people. The right place was very important to me. It still is.

It seems very clear in Scripture that Jesus had a special place. We read in the Gospels that our Lord often retreated to the Mount of Olives. There He would enter a garden and spend time alone with God and His disciples. At the moment

75

of His greatest trial it was there that He went to pray and to wait. Even Judas realized it was a special place for Jesus. When betraying our Lord, he knew just where to find Him, in the garden where He met with God.

Certainly John the Baptist had his place. It was the desert. While that does not seem like it would be my preferred spot, he lived there as a way to hear God's voice. And he was not the only one who found the wilderness a good place to experience the Lord's presence. There is clear evidence that other great saints of God went there for a time. Abraham, Moses, Elijah, Elisha and Paul all retreated to the desert for at least a while in search of God. In the third and fourth centuries hundreds of Christians went to the desert in order to find God. There, they believed, nothing could distract them from their one true love, discovering God's embrace. For them, the right place made a difference in their development. Granted, total disengagement from society can be counterproductive. But for many, days far from society's distractions can enhance their pursuit of God.

Be assured I am not suggesting that God is more in one place than another. We are not Old Testament people who must travel to some special mountain to meet with God. He is everywhere, as much present on 42nd street in New York City on a Saturday night as He is on the Northern Pacific coast at sunset. The importance of place is that it causes *you* to be more there! Special places are those which enable you to see Him better, hear His whispers and concentrate your ever-wandering mind on the glory of His magnificent being. It is just that simple. Becky Tirabassi gave very practical advice regarding "place" when she wrote,

> Have a familiar place to meet with God daily—out in the yard, at the breakfast table, at your office desk, by the garden window, or even by the fireplace. Set the atmosphere with either complete silence or soft, instrumental music. The discipline of meeting in the same place develops a consistent pattern.

> For best results, ask yourself where will you
> be the least interrupted and most comfortable for
> a specific period of time, then make that your place
> for a quiet time.[23]

Finding your "place" positions you to meet the Lord. If you are unsure, pray and ask the Lord to guide you to just the right location. Once you find it don't be surprised if it soon becomes hallowed ground, alive with His presence.

Accountability

One point in God's word is unquestionably clear. The Christian life is not to be lived in isolation. It is a shared experience of fellow pilgrims who are united by the Holy Spirit, joined by a common creed, each in pursuit of God's embrace. The very metaphors used in the New Testament support this unity. The phrases "Body of Christ," "Army of God," "People of God," "Flock of God" all point to the reality that this faith emphasizes the importance of interdependence and togetherness. Even the Greek word for church, *ecclessia*, is defined as "a people who are called out and called together."

Unity and accountability enhance spiritual well-being. When you isolate from others, the potential for distraction, deception and destruction is great. Isolation is the breeding ground for spiritual eccentricity and ill health. As such, the Lord calls you to community, where you can lovingly watch out for one another. And, when necessary, you can offer the words of instruction, correction, rebuke and even reproof that help one another stay on course with Christ. Joined together, weak and strong alike can move forward, drawing strength from each other as we all draw strength from the Lord.

Unity and accountability are an important part of positioning your life for intimacy with God. Not an easy journey, actively bonding with fellow pilgrims will help you stay focused on Him, particularly when the waves of life try to blow you off course. I recommend pursuing three types of accountability. First, if at all possible, you must become part of a community of believers that prioritizes intimacy with the Lord. Whether it is an entire local church, or a small group, this level of shared experience can be a great encouragement to your own spiritual development. I believe this commitment is most critical and, as such, am including an entire chapter to discuss the topic at the end of this book.

Secondly, try to find at least one other person who hungers for more of God and regularly challenge and encourage one another. For me, one such person is Ken Blue. For several years we have supported one another in pursuing God's embrace. Though our backgrounds and experiences are quite different, Ken and I have grown to love and respect one another. His priority is clearly that of following the heart of God. His piercing questions and deep insights have profoundly impacted my life. He has helped me regain focus repeatedly and more than once supported me when in trying times, and I have tried to do the same for him. Such relationships are critical to our lives, as indicated by that telling passage in Ecclesiastes chapter four, verses nine and ten. "Two are better than one, because they have a good return for their work. If one falls down, his friend can help him up. But pity the man who falls and has no one to help him up." If you don't have such a friend, pray for one. I believe such relationships are a priority with God and if you ask, He will provide.

Thirdly, if possible, consider finding a spiritual mentor who will help you navigate life's journey toward God's love and transforming presence. Try to locate a mature Christian man or woman who could offer you advice and encouragement. This person will serve as a spiritual father or mother, guiding you toward greater intimacy with God and increased spiritual maturity. It is best to find someone who has gone this way before you, able to point the way and offer sound counsel. In *Why Not Be a Mystic*, author Frank Tuoti comments:

> The task of direction requires discretion, prudence, a humility that does not impose one's own way

on another or allow for a desire to control others, and a profound love of the Lord illumined by one's own experiential mystical knowledge.[24]

Both Scripture and church history provide examples of spiritual mentorship. Certainly this typifies the relationship between Jesus and the disciples. He spent time teaching and modeling Kingdom life while empowering them to ably seek God and serve one another. Paul also carefully and lovingly guided Timothy toward greater intimacy with God. His love and concern come through clearly in his letters to young Timothy, revealing a deep and intimate bond between the two men. This pattern of mentorship has continued throughout church history, whether it be the example of the Desert Fathers, Christian mystics, or modern discipleship movement. The mature seek to help the novice Christian, the older and stronger reaching out to encourage the young and weak.

Again, I encourage you to pray and ask God to guide you to capable mentors. It is good to seek out men and women who are discerning, disciplined and clearly walking in the Spirit. They should be men and women who prioritize intimacy with God above all else. And he or she should be willing to lead by humble example and the force of irresistible love. This, as well as the other examples of accountability mentioned above, will serve you well. Each will help you stay focused and in place to move forward in pursuit of God and His presence.

If you want to pursue a meaningful relationship with God, radical realignment is necessary. Learning to be attentive to God's presence, scheduling quality time with Him in a place that complements intimacy, while accountable to other Christians, is a great place to start. These practical steps will properly position you toward the Lord. And when the wind of the Spirit fills the sails of healthy spiritual disciplines, an exhilarating adventure of faith and love will be underway for you.

Questions For Discussion And Review

1. What is wrong with the following statement? "If only you would pray, read Scripture, fast and serve more, you would come to know God better."

2. What is meant by the following statement? "The key to experiencing God's embrace is found in submitting to His activity. We raise the canvas of practical spiritual disciplines by faith. He sovereignly determines when to empower our efforts and to what degree."

3. If a rudder is used to position a sailing vessel towards its destination, what kinds of things position you toward the Father's embrace?

4. How does attentiveness position your life for intimacy with your Heavenly Father?

5. What did Ken Gire mean by "windows of the soul"?

6. According to Becky Tirabassi, what happens when you spend time with the Lord?

7. If you were to choose a place to meet with the Lord in devotion, what would need to be true of that location? Why?

8. Why is accountability important to positioning yourself for the journey to God's embrace?

9. What practical steps are you going to take to position yourself for God's embrace? When do you intend to do this?

Chapter Five

Learning To Set
The Sails Of Spiritual Disciplines

There was frustration in Bob's voice as he questioned me about spending time with the Lord. I was leading a seminar on the journey to God's embrace at his church and had just completed detailing my own pilgrimage toward intimacy. As often happens, the participants had mixed emotions about the topic. On the one hand they were inspired to think that such a relationship with God was even possible. They hungered for more of Him and were excited to think experiences of His presence were out there for them. On the other hand, there were frustrations and doubts as to their own ability to set aside quality time to pursue Him. Having tried and failed in the past, many were inwardly concluding that this time would probably be no different.

I saw their eyes roll as I mentioned that God had led me to spend time in daily solitude. Even though I made it clear that the length of time was not the point, the very mention of it seemed to birth discord. It was then that Bob stood to his feet, and with observable emotion said, " You must be kidding! Not only do I not have the time, I wouldn't know what to do. I fall asleep bored with fifteen or twenty minutes in prayer. What in the world would I do if I spent even more time in devotions?"

The answer to Bob's question is not all that illusive or complex. When spending time in pursuit of God, you learn to set the different sails of spiritual discipline in order to catch the wind of His Spirit. And like a sailing vessel, the more sails you lift before Him, the greater progress you will make toward His embrace. God provides the power that moves you toward intimacy through the activity of the Holy Spirit. You practice spiritual disciplines because God uses them to empower your spiritual pilgrimage.

You have already learned about positioning yourself toward His embrace through attentiveness, time, place and accountability. Now it is important that you come to understand the basic principles of spiritual formation in order to receive the empowerment of God necessary to your journey.

Spiritual Formation

I have already discussed the fact that the Christian life is a journey toward intimacy with God. And, as mentioned previously, your ongoing transformation toward Christ-likeness through purging and perfecting is a necessary part of that pilgrimage. Put simply, if you want to experience the type of relationship that Jesus had with the Father, you need to become more and more like Him. Historically, this ongoing process of transformation has been called spiritual formation.

I am thankful that this term, with its corresponding literature, is becoming increasingly popular in our day. The history and insights of this centuries-old emphasis of the Christian life is again being taken seriously. Books from people like Jeanne Guyon, Francois Fenelon, Jean-Pierre de Caussade, Saint John of the Cross, Brother Lawrence and Teresa of Avila were ignored for years by much of the evangelical community. But with the renewed interest in spiritual formation, these volumes are now complementing the more devotional classics of A. B. Simpson, Hannah Whiteall

Smith, Oswald Chambers, Andrew Murray and Jonathan Edwards ... to name a few.

Spiritual Formation Is A Process

The emphasis of all this literature is on spiritual formation. Robert Mulholland defines this term as "the process of being conformed to the image of Jesus Christ for the sake of others."[25] Notice that there are four ingredients in this definition. First, spiritual formation is a *process*. Many of us would love to find some quick fix formula for spiritual development that would fit into our "instant access" mentality. In our culture, getting something "right away" is often not soon enough. But moving toward Christ-likeness is not the result of some cosmic spiritual blast. Transformation is a process that involves seasons of change and challenge. As you surrender your life to His work you are increasingly aligned with Christ's nature and character. This opens the way to an ever-growing relationship with the Heavenly Father.

Being Conformed

Secondly, spiritual formation is the process of *being conformed*. Remember, becoming more like Christ is not the result of your efforts, but His. All you do is offer God open access to your life through surrender, constant positioning toward intimacy and the embrace of spiritual disciplines. He does the work of transforming. Instead of "Laying Hold of God," you submit to His laying hold of you, working through the "all things" of life to make you more and more like Jesus. On this journey you are not in control, He is. Your responsibility is to yield your life and efforts to His ongoing cleansing and reshaping.

The Image Of Christ

Thirdly, spiritual formation is the process of being conformed to *the image of Christ*. As you journey toward intimacy and harmony with God, He works to purge your life of the

85

"unlikeness of Christ." Every attitude, appetite and action rooted in your sinful nature is an obstacle to intimacy. God lays hold of you through what you offer Him for the purpose of making you like His Son. For example, each day you go to your special place for time with Him and pray or read the Word, you are saying, "Here, God, use this to bring to death all the 'un-Christlikeness' in my life, and increasingly fill me with His character." Every moment, every discipline, every circumstance of life can be, if you allow, an opportunity for God to work in your life. It is a way of saying, "Here, change me, God, so I might know you more."

For The Sake Of Others And Ourselves

Finally, spiritual formation is a process of being conformed to the image of Jesus Christ *for the sake of others*. At this point, I would change the definition to include "for the sake of our own lives and that of others." The journey toward Christ-likeness is, in fact, for you too. It is not selfish, nor unbiblical, to see your own development toward personal well-being as part of this process. As you change, peace and joy become realities as does growing intimacy with the Father. This is in fact the ultimate destination of your pilgrimage. Yet, it is essential to remember that the journey is not about you alone. Transformed by His presence, you are to reach out to others and invite them to join your journey to God's embrace.

Spiritual Disciplines

This brief discussion of spiritual formation will hopefully put spiritual disciplines in their proper perspective. Far too many people approach the disciplines of devotion as things "we do" to grow in Christ. When this happens, individual fortitude and determination are needed to keep devotional time going. It can birth a great deal of guilt and frustration. If your "time with God" did not go well, you may often wonder, "What did I do wrong, what could I do better?" In the end, it is increasingly easy to just not show up to the quiet place.

Spiritual disciplines play an important part in your ongoing spiritual formation. In themselves, disciplines do not change you. But, when properly submitted to God, they can become instruments of grace through which He moves to make you more and more like Jesus. You embrace them as a way of giving God room to work in your life. It is as if you are saying, "Here, God, use these to bring me to yourself," and then wait in joyful expectation. As He deems best, the Spirit will move through the discipline or disciplines you offer to draw you ever close to His presence. You do not control the coming of "the wind," but by faith you set the sails. Some days the power of His presence may be overwhelming. At other times the wind of the Spirit may not fill the sail you offer. That is His decision. Yours is but to faithfully position yourself toward intimacy and daily raise the sails of various spiritual disciplines.

What Are The Specific Spiritual Disciplines?

I want to recommend two books that give thorough treatments of this topic. Richard Foster's *Celebration of Discipline* has become a classic. He thoroughly discusses each discipline, giving helpful and practical insights on how best to approach them. I very much appreciate *The Spirit of the Disciplines* by Dallas Willard. His discussion on why a Christian should use spiritual disciplines in his or her time with God is invaluable. It lays a strong foundation for building these practices into our lives.

It is helpful to place the spiritual disciplines in two categories: Those which focus on giving up something, and those which enable us to receive. Willard identifies these as the disciplines of abstinence and the disciplines of engagement. What follows is a necessarily brief definition of each discipline according to their appropriate categorization.

Disciplines of Abstinence
Solitude: Choosing to come apart from our daily activity in order to be alone with God.

Silence: In silence we choose against the noise of the world and self in order to listen to the whispers of God.

Fasting: Abstaining from food for a specific period of time in order to lessen the grip our flesh has upon our lives and open the way to experience God's strength in weakness.

Frugality: In a world of material excess, we choose to say no to luxuries and wants, focusing upon God as our satisfaction in life.

Chastity: Choosing to set aside, for a season, the sexual aspect of the marriage relationship in order to concentrate on spiritual union. An abstinence in marriage demands mutual consent.

Secrecy: Consciously choosing to follow the admonition of Jesus and do our deeds of service and giving in private.

Sacrifice: Giving beyond our ability in response to God's self-giving and as a means to enhance trust in our lives.

Disciplines of Engagement
Study: Choosing to spend time meditating upon the Word of God. The goal of this discipline is not acquiring information, but allowing God to spiritually form our lives.

Worship: This means to declare the wonder and supreme worth of God, engaging our hearts, minds, soul and body in an ongoing offering of adoration.

Celebration: Choosing to find and experience joy in the life God gives us, celebrating the goodness of the created order in all its beauty and greatness.

Service: Engaging our lives, resources, talents and spiritual gifts in ministry to others. We accept Jesus' example of servanthood through the towel and basin.

Prayer: Through the power of the Holy Spirit, we are able to commune with God through prayer as well as affect the world around us and the spiritual reality through our requests and petitions.

Fellowship: Choosing to integrate actively into the healthy, spiritual community, as a place of united strength, increased faith and demonstrated love.

Confession: Jesus works through our weakness and brings us wholeness as we bring all things into the light. This discipline involves opening up our broken hearts before one another for mutual strength and support.

Submission: Choosing to come under the authority and direction of those in anointed spiritual leadership. This discipline also involves seeking out spiritual directors who help guide us toward Christ-likeness.

Where Should A Person Start?

With all these disciplines, how are you to choose? In time you will learn two important truths about finding just the right disciplines for your ongoing spiritual development. First, many of these address specific places of rebellion and weakness in your life. For example, if struggling with selfishness and greed, you would do well to offer God the "sails" of sacrifice and service. As you do, He will unleash the wind of the Spirit to move you toward change. Secondly, you can pray and ask the Lord to guide you to particular disciplines. He will answer by quickening your heart to those that best serve your place in the journey toward intimacy.

I would like to recommend a simple starting place for you. Having positioned yourself toward God's embrace, consistently include these three disciplines in your pursuit; worship, prayer and Scripture reading. I believe these activities regularly give room for God to move upon your life and draw you closer to Himself. In time you can and should grow to include other channels of grace. But here is, in my opinion, the best place to begin. What follows is a brief practical discussion of these three disciplines.

Worship And Praise

The Bible clearly teaches that praise and worship are to be a holy preoccupation for God's people. Virtually everywhere you turn in Scripture, the admonition to exalt the Lord is there, calling Christians to lift heart and hand and voice before the Lord. Whether by spoken word, or song, or even dance, a continuous offering of worship is to ascend from your life to His throne. Certainly this discipline of God's grace needs to be part of your regular time in the quiet place with Him. And let me tell you why.

Because He Is Worthy
First and foremost, worship and praise God because He is worthy and infinitely indescribable. His character is holy and above reproach and His creation is magnificent. His act of redemption is an unbelievable display of love and grace. His provision for your life is complete and abundant. Regardless of your situation or lot in life, God is deserving of your utmost in praise and adoration because He is majestic and mighty in all He does. To lift your heart and hands before Him in worship is a sacrifice you make simply because He is God, mysterious, powerful and great.

Praise Unleashes His Presence
Secondly, you are to worship and praise God because it consistently unleashes His presence in your life. You can experience this in both private times of devotion and corporate gatherings. Something dynamic happens when your

90

praise ascends toward the Father. It is as if worship and adoration opens a doorway to heaven, and His presence begins to pour down from above. I have seen churches radically transformed by the electrifying presence of God because they wholeheartedly offered Him a sacrifice of praise. I have listened as Christians testify to personal renewal and restoration by prioritizing worship. Personally, praise opens my spirit to His glorious presence as little else, initiating feelings of awe and deep wonder. I seem to come alive deep within with overflowing love and gratefulness. If you long for His presence, praise is definitely a sail you need to set.

A Weapon Against Evil

Thirdly, praise pushes back the evil one from your midst. The reality of Satan's efforts to deceive and destroy should be obvious to you. He is hell-bent on wrecking your life and through his demonic horde, active at every turn. You, however, are far from defenseless. Jesus has provided you with armor and weapons of defense. Praise and worship are a powerful part of that arsenal.

In 2 Chronicles 20 we read of how praise defeated the Ammorite and Moabite armies. God positioned Israel on the mountain heights and told them to declare His glory. He then went into the valley and conquered their enemies. The Bible says, "As they began to sing praise, the Lord set ambushes against the men of Ammon and Moab and Mount Seir who were invading Judah, and they were defeated" (2 Chronicles 20:22). Praise holds that same power today. Whenever you lift His glory, the darkness of the evil one subsides. Given Satan's constant barrage against you, praise should become a way of life for you.

The wonder of His glory, the hunger for His presence and the need for His intervention against evil are three powerful reasons to prioritize praise and worship . You do well to include this mighty discipline in your daily time before the Lord. You can do this by:

Listening to praise music in an attitude of adoration.
There are countless CD's and cassettes that contain wonderful praise music. Find the best of these and bring them into your quite time.

Singing favorite choruses or hymns. These ageless songs tell the story of grace as little else and can center you in God's truth and promises.

Giving thanks to God for His blessings, such as salvation in Christ, the Person of the Holy Spirit, daily provision, answers to prayer and so forth. There is spiritual power when you choose to give thanks to God for all that He has done and is doing in your life. Burdens are lifted and perspective is refocused upon the goodness of God in even the most difficult of times.

Worshiping the Lord according to the specific qualities of His character, such as His holiness, grace, benevolence, power, love, patience, righteousness, compassion, faithfulness, sovereignty and constant presence. I have found it so filling to choose one of the above and then quietly meditate on all that it means, allowing the Holy Spirit to quicken me deep within, initiating deep adoration and praise.

Hebrews 13:15 calls you to "continually offer to God a sacrifice of praise." Incorporating these few suggestions into your time with the Lord is an excellent way to begin fulfilling this command. Praise is a discipline God seems always to bless, using it to move you ever closer to His loving presence. Allow the cry of your heart to overflow in song before the Lord. You will soon be caught up into His presence, and I assure you that you will want to go to that special place every single day.

Prayer

John Wesley once said that "God will do nothing but in answer to prayer." The further I go on my Christian journey, the more I understand the truth of what he said. Prayer is a channel of God's grace that consistently brings about change on this earth. And you would do well to embrace it as a foundational discipline of Christian discipleship. Prayer enables you to call for God's involvement in the events of the world around you. And it is a means of intimate communion with the Father. Tuoti writes:

> Without a discipline of prayer, without extended intervals of silence and solitude in our busy lives, contemplation will remain an unrealized sentiment. The living waters come to us over the aqueduct of prayer. As soon as we make the commitment to a prayer discipline, our lives begin to change almost immediately, for the waters of grace come quickly trickling down.[26]

Jesus prayed. All you need to do is read the Gospels and learn how important it was to His life. Whenever Jesus was under pressure, making decisions, or facing opposition, betrayal and death, He prayed. It was such an obvious part of His daily relationship with God that His disciples asked Him to teach them about this discipline. They in turn modeled the importance of prayer before their followers, instructing them to do likewise. Specific New Testament commands regarding prayer include:

Pray continually.	1 Thessalonians 5:16, 17
Devote yourselves to prayer.	Colossians 4:2
Pray about everything in a spirit of rejoicing.	Philippians 4:6-8
Pray in the Spirit.	Ephesians 6:18
Pray on all occasions.	Ephesians 6:18
Pray for each other.	James 5:16
Pray for open doors.	Colossians 4:3

These are but a small sampling of the many Scriptures that instruct you to spend time before the Lord in prayer. The vast number of references that speak to this discipline can lead you to only one conclusion. You must pray! It is a channel of His grace, a place to meet Him in petition and fellowship. Time devoted to prayer is time wisely invested in your pursuit of His embrace.

Admit That Praying Is Difficult For You

Where should you begin with prayer? It may well start with a confession that you have difficulty praying. Frankly, that was the prayer that changed my prayer life. I opened up before God and honestly admitted my own frailty. I told Him that I had trouble focusing, wandered in my thoughts and at times fell asleep while trying to pray. I then asked Him for help and committed to "setting my sail" daily in anticipation of His empowerment. The result: my entire attitude, appetite and aptitude for prayer was transformed. Prayer has become one of my favorite places to meet God. While I am still known to doze off at times, I have learned to daily turn to the Spirit and ask for help, and things consistently begin to happen.

Develop Your Own Prayer Outline

It is also helpful to have a pattern for prayer, or as the saints of old referred to it, "a rule of prayer." It serves as a navigational map to keep you on course. First, as mentioned previously, spend time in praise, worship and thanks. Come to God recognizing the power of the blood of Christ and thanking Him for your adoption as His child. This will give you confidence to move toward God with expectation and boldness. Next, spend time meditating on the various names of Christ Jesus found in the New Testament. These include:
Shepherd, 1 Peter 5:2
Bridegroom, Revelation 19:6-8
Bread of Life, John 6:35

Lamb of God, John 1:36
Prince of Peace, Isaiah 9:6
Suffering Servant, Isaiah 53
Lion, Revelation 5:5
Immanuel, Matthew 1:23
Lord, Philippians 2:11
Jesus, Matthew 1:21

Each metaphor is rich in meaning. By meditating on them, you will grow to know Christ better. Try to picture each image in your mind, worshipping Jesus in the wonder of His majesty and power. When possible, stay here for long periods, being caught up in the presence of your wonderful Lord and Savior.

From here you can move on to bring before the Lord specific requests for those closest to you. These prayers should focus most on issues of spiritual growth and development. You may want to keep a list of specific items of concern after each of your names, daily lifting them before the Lord one by one. Once complete, move on to seek God's help for the various needs and provisions necessary to your life. Every day, you can pray about matters of finance, health and practical concerns. Jesus taught this in His prayer model, and I believe it is an invitation to seek God's constant intervention.

Next, come before the Lord both to seek forgiveness of sin and to extend forgiveness to any who have offended you. In 1 John 1:9, you are assured that Jesus is ready and willing to forgive you. You need only confess your sin and He will purify you of all unrighteousness. It is good daily to ask the Holy Spirit to reveal both the root and fruit of your failings. As He does, move to confess each offense by faith, trusting on His grace to forgive. It is also important to be just as forgiving to those who have sinned against you. Remember that His mercy toward you should overflow to those around you.

After this, I suggest that you pray "on" each piece of the armor of God listed in Ephesians 6. Each piece represents some truth vital to our victory over evil.

The Belt of Truth — a declaration that God's Word is the only truth you need for spiritual health.

The Breastplate of Righteousness — a declaration of your new identity in Christ and standing before God as His holy child.

The Shoes of the Gospel of Peace — a readiness to embrace and communicate the good news of reconciliation through the blood of Christ.

The Shield of Faith — a declaration of trust in God regardless of circumstances.

The Helmet of Salvation — the symbol of victory and hope.

The Sword of the Spirit — God's living word that specifically addresses the harassment and deception of Satan.

Next, be encouraged to spend time interceding for various people and ministries. You may want to place some people on your list permanently, while others are there only during times of special need.

Finally, and most importantly, sit and listen! Ask God to speak to your heart about any and all issues pertinent to your life. Wait in quiet to see if there are special concerns He would have you lift in prayer, or prophetic insights He wants you to receive. As you silently pray in the Spirit, contemplate His love and soak in His presence. At times fill your mind with some meditative phrase, such as "The Lord is my Shepherd," or "I am His beloved." This can be, more often than not, a time of intimate communion, direction and delight. All else will seem to fade as the wonder of God's truth enlightens your inner being. Such times of quiet union will soon be the place you long for most and where you stay the longest. I believe this silent communing is the highest and richest expression of the life of prayer, presenting a most satisfying harmony between you and the Father of love.

Once again I would recommend two books which are helpful in developing a meaningful prayer life. The first is Richard Foster's *Prayer: Finding the Heart's True Home* and the classic by Ole Hallesby, simply titled, *Prayer*. Both will enrich your understanding of this most critical spiritual discipline.

Scripture

The Bible is a priceless and multifaceted gift given by God to His people. It provides the foundation of everything you need to know as a Christian. It is a divine guidebook regarding every essential matter of faith and Christian living. Through stories, poetry, parables and principles, the Bible points the way to God, from sinful darkness to your glorious adoption into His eternal family. Scripture unveils the centrality of Jesus Christ to life and invites you to follow Him toward ever-increasing oneness with God. And as if that were not enough, every word of Scripture is alive with the presence of God, through the Holy Spirit. Regularly read the Bible, bringing it into your time of devotion and quiet virtually every day.

Ask The Spirit to Help You

Let me suggest some practical ways to make approaching Scripture part of your pursuit of God's embrace. As with prayer, you will do well to begin by asking God for help. Many Christians find reading Scripture difficult. Frankly, I believe this is a spiritual issue best addressed by turning to the Holy Spirit. I frequently pray for people, asking God to give them a renewed hunger for His word. Invariably, this prayer of faith ignites a new passion to read the Bible.

Use A Readable Version Of Scripture

Second, it is best to use a version of the Bible that is easy to understand. I recognize there has been a long-standing controversy about which version is the correct one to use. My answer is simple. Choose the one that is easiest to read. I prefer the *New International Version*. But other versions, like the *New King James*, *New American Standard*, and *New Revised Standard* are all good translations. Paraphrases, like the *New*

Living Bible and *The Message* are extremely helpful for believers. You should feel free to find the Bible that fits you best.

Let God Transform You Through His Word

Thirdly, approach Scripture with the goal of meeting God there. Granted, there is a place for detailed informational Bible study. Yet it is not the best use of Scripture in devotional time. Your head can be filled with knowledge, yet your heart untouched by His presence. Come to Scripture with a view to experiencing His touch deep within. The following additional steps to reading Scripture will open the way to His presence.

Allow The Spirit To Inspire Your Heart

Approach God's word sensitive to the inspiration of the Holy Spirit. It is good to pray, "Holy Spirit, what do you want to show me in Scripture today? Quicken my heart to recognize your presence in and through the verses I read. Form and shape me by my encounter with you in the Word of God." Such an approach gives room for God to impact your heart, not just your mind. A powerful book dedicated exclusively to this topic is Robert Mulholland's *Shaped By the Word*. I heartily recommend it if you are pursuing more of God's presence in your life.

Move Slowly

Next, read the Scriptures slowly. The goal of formational reading is encountering God, not devouring whole chapters at one sitting. It is best to read only a few verses at a time, contemplating their meaning and application for your life. For example, recently I meditated on John 19:15. It is the passage where the crowd cries, "Crucify Him," and the declaration of the chief priests, "We have no king but Caesar." These righteous leaders wanted Jesus dead and made a deal with the devil to get it. Meditating on this event led me to ask God to reveal compromise in my own life, and purge me of any manipulative ways of "getting what I want." It was a powerful moment in His presence. I did not cover much Scripture, but it certainly covered and conquered me!

Read Systematically

I also wholeheartedly recommend reading Scripture systematically. Bible roulette is seldom an effective way to approach God's word. It is far better to read through a book verse by verse. This not only gives you a broader exposure to His word, but it builds you up in Christ block by block. I find it helpful to include some sections of a Gospel in daily reading. Doing this will keep the life of Christ constantly before you and over time shape your own approach to life in this fallen world. Looking at Jesus every day will affect the way you see the people and events around you.

Allow The Lord Access To Your Imagination

Finally, you will unlock the door to God's presence by reading Scripture with a sanctified imagination. You do well to allow the Holy Spirit access to your imagination, helping you visualize the particular truth or event being contemplated in God's word. It may be valuable for you to begin with a brief prayer, asking the Spirit to cleanse and control your mind for this purpose. This approach opens you to the Lord in ways that go beyond the mind, engaging the senses and emotions at deep levels. Mulholland recommends this technique as a key for formational reading. He writes,

> You imagine the feelings you would be seeing … the things you would be hearing …, smelling … feeling. You use all your senses. You let your imagination loose to recreate the setting of the passage of Scripture.[27]

Asking the Holy Spirit to help you "enter" a passage will reap unbelievable fruit in your relationship with God. You will see and understand truths in His word more deeply than ever before.

I highly recommend these steps to reading Scripture. They will help you when seeking to experience more of God, empowering you to turn full into the wind of His presence and move forward to increasing intimacy with Him.

Spiritual disciplines are important to your journey. They give the Lord open access to your life, serving as channels of His transforming presence. The disciplines of worship and praise, prayer and Scripture are a great place to start. Once under way, you will learn to set other sails that will help you travel with even greater force. Each discipline can be a unique and exciting instrument of the Holy Spirit's work of spiritual formation. Several of these disciplines have profoundly affected my life. Fasting, service, sacrifice, confession and fellowship have been used by the Lord to change me forever. But this book is about beginnings, and I fear too much, too soon will lead to fear and frustration. And so I am trusting that, in this case, less is truly more.

I realize this discussion has been brief, but hopefully it will begin to answer the question, "How should I spend time before the Lord in quiet and devotion?" If you do these things in the way suggested I believe two things will happen. First, you will experience His presence, which is your greatest priority and privilege. And secondly, no matter how much time you are spending with the Lord, it soon won't seem like enough! God is inviting you toward His embrace and the wind is blowing. May you position yourself toward His loving arms and set sail.

Questions For Discussion And Review

1. What is spiritual formation?

2. What is meant by the following?
Spiritual formation as a process . . .

Of being conformed . . .

To the image of Christ . . .

For our lives and others . . .

3. What role do spiritual disciplines play in this process?

4. What is a discipline of abstinence? Engagement?

5. What are the reasons for incorporating praise and worship into your devotional times?

6. How could a person practically include praise and worship in daily quiet before the Lord?

7. In what way does an outline for prayer help you?

8. What would be a good outline for your prayer time? Develop one that you could use.

9. What is the difference between an informational and formational reading of Scripture?

10. What is the best way to approach Scripture formationally? How could you best appropriate this into your time before the Lord?

Chapter Six

The Call To Community

We had already been together on retreat for three days, focusing on the priority of intimacy with God. There were twelve participants, men and women who were desperately hungry for more of the Father. They came from a variety of backgrounds, but with a single focus. They wanted to learn how to experience more of God's presence in their daily lives. Leading them through the various topics regarding the journey to God's embrace was a joy. Their enthusiasm made teaching a delight. By the way they responded it seemed that every session was exciting and inspiring. It was like serving starving people their first cooked meal in weeks, watching them devour the food with reckless enthusiasm.

At virtually every session, the participants hurriedly took notes, asked good, leading questions, and entered into the contemplative disciplines and symbolic activities with abandon. Most everything that was said and done hit a sympathetic chord within their hearts. But without question, the note that brought the greatest response was the one sounded on the importance of community.

I began to talk about the relationship between community and the pursuit of intimacy with God on the morning of the third day. It was immediately evident that this topic had engaged them quite emotionally. There was a dynamic tension to their inquiries and responses relative to the topic. On the one hand, they seemed thoroughly convinced that being in deep, intimate relationship with other believers was essential to their spiritual development. But they also voiced frustration that such genuine friendships were hard to find and develop in the contemporary evangelical church.

Suddenly Janie began to cry. All eyes turned in her direction as I asked her if we could help. She struggled through tears to talk about her loneliness, her isolation and her sense of abandonment. Janie said that she desperately wanted intimate friendships, yet was tired of knocking on door after door, only to find no one there for her. And to hear me say that true community was essential to her growth in the Lord only compounded her heartache.

It was obvious that many in the room shared Janie's feelings. They all voiced, in their own way, the fact that they were not experiencing true community in their lives, were genuinely desiring such an experience of corporate life and were frustrated because they did not know where to start. For the next two days, the call to community was the center of our time together.

Life Together Enhances Intimacy

I believe these twelve people are representative of the heart cry of Christians everywhere. The life of faith is to be a shared experience, not an exercise in isolation and independence. While times of solitude are undoubtedly essential to your spiritual growth, participating in community is equally vital to wholeness and well being. Each serves to keep you balanced and properly centered to grow in the Lord. As such, the call to Christ is equally a summons to enter genuine community.

Brennan Manning writes quite pointedly about the importance of community in *The Signature of Jesus.*

> A second characteristic of paschal spirituality is
> that it is aware of the community of God's people.

We belong to God's people. Christianity can never be an affair that simply embraces our individual happiness. Paschal spirituality avoids an exaggerated form of Christian individualism — a "Jesus and me" mentality. God did not call us into salvation in isolation but in community. Our personal destiny is but part of his magnificent saving plan that includes in its sweep not only the entire human community but the whole of creation, the inauguration of the new heavens and the new earth. The Jesus-and-me mindset tells us that all we have to do is accept Christ as Savior, read the Bible, go to church, and save our souls. Christianity becomes simply a telephone booth affair, a private conversation between God and me without reference to my brothers and sisters. I go to church on Sunday while the world goes to hell. When preoccupation with my personal salvation drugs me into such insensitivity that I no longer hear the bleating of the lost sheep, then Karl Marx was right: Religion is the opiate of the people... The Christian life is meant to be lived in community. And community life is a radical imitation of the holy and undivided Trinity who is dialogue, spontaneous love, and relationship.[28]

Manning's point resonates with the entire testimony of scripture. To love God, you must spend time growing with His people.

God's Word Calls You Into Community

Even a casual glance at Scripture confirms that the life of faith is not an experience in autonomy and isolation. Consider if you will, the essential nature of belonging in the Israelite culture of Old Testament times. A high priority was placed on an individual's being connected to the greater community. Israelite men, women or children identified and defined themselves in relationship to their place in the family, clan, tribe and nation. Genealogies were detailed as a way of indicating place and relationship to people of the past, present and future. While people were valued as individuals, it was their inter-relatedness that mattered most. If a person violated that commitment to community well being, drastic action was in order. Nowhere is this seen more clearly than in the story of Achan in Joshua, chapter seven.

Having compromised the safety of family, clan, tribe and nation he was summarily executed. In a highly individualistic society such as ours, it is difficult to understand such drastic actions. But in a culture where interdependence was highly valued, individual rights were secondary to community health and safety. No one Israelite was permitted to put the entire society at risk by his or her attitudes or actions.

Jesus clearly modeled and taught that life together was essential to pursuing God. The Gospel record gives ample evidence that our Lord lived and ministered in the context of genuine community. He had close, open and loving relationships with James, John and Peter, and the other disciples, as well as intimate friendships with people like Lazarus and his sisters Mary and Martha. While faithful to spend time in solitude, Jesus also prioritized time with the people He loved. He would teach them, listen to their concerns, share His feelings and thoughts, and impart life to them on a regular basis. Our Lord moved from time alone with God, to experiences of shared life, to withdrawal once again. This balance undoubtedly impacted His life and ministry significantly, an example to you and me that pursuing God is not an either/ or, but a both/and embrace of solitude and community.

In the hours before Christ went to the cross alone, He taught and ministered to the community of His closest followers. They were together as Jesus washed their feet, together as He celebrated the Passover, together as He spoke to them of loving each other and together as He prayed and was arrested in Gethsemane. Most of the post-resurrection appearances of Christ came as the disciples were gathered together, as well as the ascension and outpouring of the Holy Spirit at Pentecost. There can be no denying that "life together" was indispensable to knowing and growing in their experience of God.

With the birth of the New Testament church at Pentecost, the followers of Christ were drawn together in a clearly defined experience of community. Luke's description found in Acts portrays a committed and interdependent people joined in a common pursuit for more of God. He writes:

> *They devoted themselves to the apostles' teaching and to the fellowship, to the breaking of bread and to prayer. Everyone was filled with awe, and many wonders and miraculous signs were done by the apostles. All the believers were together and had everything in common. Selling their possessions and goods, they gave to anyone as he had need. Every day they continued to meet together in the temple courts. They broke bread in their homes and ate together with glad and sincere hearts, praising God and enjoying the favor of all the people. And the Lord added to their number daily those who were being saved.* — Acts 2:43-47

The ingredients for shared life are all there, including worship, teaching, serving, sharing and praising God, together. The first century path to spiritual growth and intimacy with God included, unquestionably, a commitment to corporate solidarity and servanthood.

The Apostle Paul repeatedly emphasized the communal dimension of faith in his letters, particularly with use of the "body metaphor" as it relates to Christ's church. He addresses this theme in his epistles to the Romans, Ephesians and his first letter to the church in Corinth. Paul wanted believers to understand that each individual is part of a larger fellowship of Christ's followers, mutually dependent and interrelated. Spiritual growth, to Paul, was to occur within the context of community life and experience. He is not negating individual encounters with Christ, but rather identifying the fact that personal faith is to be rooted, grounded

107

and developed in the context of genuine Christian community. He writes:

> *Just as each of us has one body with many members, and these members do not all have the same function, so in Christ we who are many form one body, and each member belongs to all the others.*
>
> — Romans 12:4, 5

> *Consequently, you are no longer foreigners and aliens, but fellow citizens with God's people and members of God's household, built on the foundation of the apostles and prophets, with Christ Jesus himself as the chief cornerstone. In him the whole building is joined together and rises to become a holy temple in the Lord. And in him you too are being built together to become a dwelling in which God lives by his Spirit.*
>
> — Ephesians 2:19-22

> *From him the whole body, joined and held together by every supporting ligament, grows and builds itself up in love, as each part does its work.*
>
> — Ephesians 4:16

> *The body is a unit, though it is made up of many parts; and though all its parts are many, they form one body. So it is with Christ. For we were all baptized by one Spirit into one body — whether Jews or Greeks, slave or free — and we were all given the one Spirit to drink.*
>
> — 1 Corinthians 12:12, 13

John picks up this topic in his first epistle, under the theme of love. After describing the lavish love of the Father, expressed in the sacrifice of Christ, and poured out on believers in countless ways, he challenges Christians to love one another. John tells his readers that God's great love for them should empower and motivate deep expressions of love for each other. He goes so far as to challenge believers with the fact that the absence of such love brings into question the validity of one's declaration of faith and love for the Father. He writes:

> We love because he first loved us. If anyone says, "I love God," yet hates his brother, he is a liar. For anyone who does not love his brother, whom he has seen, cannot love God, whom he has not seen. And he has given us this command: Whoever loves God must also love his brother.
> — 1 John 4:19-21

Christian people down through the centuries have endeavored to respond to the scriptural call to community in many different ways. In the first century house churches were formed as places of fellowship, support, worship and servanthood. By the third and fourth centuries, people began to retreat to the desert where mentoring relationships were formed, combining solitude and corporate life as disciplines vital to experiencing God. In the middle ages, monasteries were born with hopes of balancing private and communal expressions of faith. By the eighteenth century small groups, under men like Whitefield and Wesley, took shape and were key in evangelizing and discipling hundreds of thousands of Christian people. Here, at the dawn of the twenty-first century, all these expressions of shared life, and many more, are to be found throughout the world. Imperfect as they all may be, the goal of each expression of community life is rooted in the admonition of our Lord to love one another, as He has loved his people (John13:34).

The Characteristics Of True Community

What should you look for when seeking out genuine community? What ingredients are essential to spiritual well-being, and which are not? Will any gathering of Christians fulfill that role in your life, regardless of size or structure? What common commitments and beliefs are necessary among participants to ensure health and balance in the corporate experience? The answers to these and several other questions are very important if you are to grow in Christian community as the Lord intends. What follows are nine characteristics that I believe are foundational and, I might add, non-negotiable to shared life in genuine Christ-centered fellowship. Where found and developed, you will most certainly find yourself growing more like Christ and ever close to God's sweet embrace. Without them, you risk participating in a corporate experience that is open to imbalance and immaturity at best, and at its worst personal harm.

But before identifying what genuine Christian community looks like, let's be sure to recognize and accept what it is not. We Christians are human beings with weaknesses, flaws and countless imperfections. You and I make mistakes, often by accident and sometimes quite intentionally. Any notion that life together will be fail-safe is unreasonable. There will be all the ups and downs that come with connecting with sinful men and women who are struggling to be free in Christ. Getting "it" right the first time all the time can not be an expectation placed on individuals within the community. Your focus must be on progress along the way, not resting secure at the final destination!

Sabrina, a woman who has some difficulty in forming lasting friendships, was a participant at the retreat mentioned earlier. As the discussion began regarding the necessary shared commitments for successful community, she revealed some very unhealthy biases. Sabrina told us that she did not want to be with people who smoke, drink, have unruly children, can't be depended on or trusted completely. She probably shared more concerns, but my mind quickly lost focus.

As she talked my thoughts went to the Lord's community. One member was inconsistent (Peter), another a revolutionary rebel (Simon the Zealot), another a conspirator (Matthew), two struggled with bad tempers (James and John) and one was a traitor (Judas). Hands down they did not have it all together going in, did they? Yet each said yes to Jesus and under His leadership transformation took place over time (except for Judas). They probably would have not been welcome in Sabrina's fellowship. Yet these imperfect saints are far more characteristic of most of us than we would like to admit. Jesus saw in them what I believe He sees in you and me: What we can become! The key to their, and our, inclusion centers on a willingness to grow beyond where they were to where the Lord wanted them to be. Potential, not perfection, is the bottom line for all of us. It is not where you are, but where you and the other members of your community are willing to go that counts most.

The characteristics of community that I will be sharing have been drawn from the life and ministry of the Lord. While there are several good resources that suggest principles for healthy relationships, Scripture is the primary source for living the Christian life as intended. By considering Jesus and His interaction with those closest to Him, you will discover the commitments necessary to a transforming experience in community. I will in some cases choose to illustrate or support the point being discussed by referring to other books and resources. But the model that will truly draw you closer to God and his people is found in the Gospel accounts of the Lord's days here on earth.

A Called-Out Community

The first characteristic of genuine Christian community is that it's members have been called out by Christ to leave what is familiar and safe, embarking on a journey to a new way of life. Read the Gospels and you will see that this was true of the Lord's disciples. Peter, James and John were called away from their nets. Matthew was summoned by the Lord to leave his tax table, and Simon the Zealot had to lay down his revolutionary activities and embrace the way of peace. To be truly confronted by Kingdom realities, the normal, comfortable, risk-free contexts of their lives had to be shaken. And so Jesus called the apostles out.

The message of the Gospels is the same for you, isn't it? The words of Christ call you to come apart from family and friends, and the routine of your normal schedule of duties and delights, in order to experience life as God intended. While this may not mean a change of location or vocation, the "calling out" of Christ does mean leaving your comfort zone to encounter God in an environment without your normal safety nets.

Being "called out" means placing yourself among a group of people who will be honest, vulnerable, compassionate, and at times confrontational. It means leaving behind the coping mechanisms and behaviors that keep you safely hidden away, coming forth as you truly are, in all your God-given strengths and debilitating weaknesses. It means being called out from your defended fortress, and standing naked, open and at risk. Such experiences will not be warm, fuzzy or safe. But this calling out will change you forever. It will enable you to connect with people and their brokenness like never before. And being called out will position you to know and love God above all else. Only those in community who have been courageous enough to leave the old ways behind will be able to journey to the new place of spiritual life and vitality.

A Called-Together Community

While Jesus extended the call to follow him individually, He did not leave each person to experience Him in isolation or solitude. Instead, He brought them all into the community of His followers. They were not only called out, but also called together in Him. The very word for church, *ekklesia*, means "a people who have been called out and called together." Christians are called out from the sinful, broken ways of the world and called together in order to develop personally as well as to grow in love for God and one another.

Being "called together" does not mean all people in your community should share the same interests, be at the identical place in their pilgrimage as you, or have excised from their lives all annoying idiosyncrasies and habits. I am quite sure that the odd collection of personalities our Lord gathered

112

around himself made for some tense and challenging times. Can you imagine what it must have been like to have a revolutionary zealot (Simon) and a Roman collaborator (Matthew) in the same intimate community?

Being "called together" means that you are joining with several other imperfect people, endeavoring to live out the gospel of love in very specific and concrete ways. It means leaving your comfort zone and moving forward to experience Kingdom life "together," trusting that the uniqueness of each person will be used by Christ to draw every fellow traveler closer to the purposes and presence of God. Being "called together" is very much about sensing that the Lord, by the Holy Spirit, has brought you to one another for a season of deep growth and spiritual development. You will realize that it was God who has gathered you to be shoulder to shoulder on the journey.

<u>A Christ-Centered Community</u>

For you to experience true Christian community, Jesus Christ must be at the very center of your shared life. He should be the Object of your worship, the Example you all seek to follow, the Teacher you learn from in life, the Savior you each trust, and the Master you obey and serve. By the power of His indwelling Holy Spirit you should encourage each other to live as He lived, think as He thought and love as Jesus loved. You must reject the self-centered way of the world and embrace the power of the Christ-life.

This preoccupation with the person of Jesus Christ is clearly taught and modeled in the Gospel narratives. Jesus called men and women to follow Him (Matthew 9:19), leave all to be with Him (Mark 10:2) and even carry a cross in response to His love (Luke 14:27). He told His disciples that no person or thing should take precedence over loving Him and obeying His commands (Luke 14:26). And these men and women certainly gave all in response to Christ, even to the point of persecution and death. The disciples knew that He and He alone had the words of eternal life, and as such they submitted to Jesus Christ as their Lord (John 6:68, 69).

113

Your community of fellow travelers is called to be faithful in keeping all eyes and thoughts on Christ. He is to be the focus of your songs, your conversation, your learning and your life. Your faith is not based on a religion of rules and regulations, but a relationship with the living Lord. That intimate embrace needs to be consistently at the very heart of your time together. He and He alone is the Way, the Truth and the Life (John14:6), and as such you must be diligent to keep Him at the very center of your community.

A Compassionate Community

One of the most powerful and moving stories in Scripture is that of the woman caught in adultery (John 8:1-11). It is an account full of human emotion and ugly accusation, but also an illustration of the true compassion God intends Christians to extend to one another and to a broken world. Here is a woman caught in the very act of adultery, a sin justifiably punishable by death. But Jesus shows the community a quality far more powerful than justice. He extends compassion to her and as a result she is changed forever.

The crowd of religious zealots and Pharisees confronted Jesus with the sinful woman to see if He would do the right thing, which to their minds was execution. Instead, the Lord confronts them with their own moral culpability by inviting only the sinless to throw stones. Exposed, they walked away in silence. To the woman, Jesus extended only forgiveness and the call to holy living.

In genuine Christian community you strive to show compassion to the sinful and broken in your midst. The basis of this compassion is two fold. First, you and every member are to admit honestly that every one stands on level ground before Christ — sinful. You do well to recognize humbly that there is no sin another has committed that you are not capable of doing. And secondly, from this basis you are to extend true forgiveness without judgment or condemnation. Such compassion incarnates the true spirit of Christ within your community, enhancing love, intimacy and the pursuit of holy living.

A Confessing Community

I am often struck by the honesty and openness of the first century Christian community, particularly in respect to their weaknesses and failures. Read the Gospels and you find no whitewashing or pretense when it comes to sin. You are told that James and John had explosive tempers. Peter's shallow boastings and his denial of Christ are presented in detail. And Thomas' skepticism and doubt are neither sugar-coated nor explained away. You find that these saints were real people, with all the inconsistencies and imperfections found in Christians today.

Their willingness to confess openly and own their sinfulness was, I believe, because of the non-condemning attitude of Christ. Certainly not soft on sin (after all, Jesus died to cleanse people from its effects), Jesus was loving and encouraging to the sinner. He was generous to forgive and gave His followers more than a second chance. As long as they returned to Him in repentance, Jesus offered nothing but grace and mercy.

Most Christians are very hesitant to confess openly and be vulnerable in community. Fearing rejection, judgment and gossip, broken people often choose to struggle alone. However, this forced isolation only sets them up for deeper trouble, for the battle against evil demands both help and loving accountability.

Growing in Christ and moving toward intimacy demands that you are part of a community of people who are safe. This means that you and they work to be a non-condemning, non-judgmental, confidential gathering of imperfect saints. You strive to be honest about your struggles within the confines of the group, in order to receive the help and support so necessary to freedom and victory. In such a place, you are free to confess your failures all the while knowing that every person in community is a fellow traveler longing to receive the grace that heals.

A Caring Community

Michael Card has written a powerful song about the call to community. It is titled "The Basin and the Towel," and, as the title suggests, it focuses on the story of Jesus washing the disciples' feet in the upper room. His point in the song is that Jesus shows us all how to connect with one another: by caring enough to touch broken people and serve them with tender love. Card summons believers to enter true Christian community by following the example of our Lord and bowing low to serve each other as Jesus did.

Over and over again Jesus connected with people by caring. Whether it was by sitting with tax collectors and sinners, healing the sick, feeding the hungry or weeping with the broken, our Lord entered into the pain and suffering of others and served them in love. He did not minister from a safe and respectable distance, but identified completely with the people who came His way. Though many reacted to His actions with contempt, Jesus would not be controlled by cultural or religious proprieties. And what He did for His community, He calls you to do as well.

Caring that is translated into costly servanthood is a necessary ingredient of Christian community. You are encouraged to take risks in order to demonstrate the love of Christ when people are in need. You are not to serve because it makes you feel good, or because you think it somehow gives you advanced status with God. You serve because it helps people who hurt, and connects them with the God who loves them so dearly. Such caring will open the way to levels of intimacy with people and God that is simply transforming.

A Confrontive Community

While Jesus showed great love and patience with the weaknesses of His disciples, He also would confront them when necessary. Whether it was their lack of faith or fear or stubborn behaviors, the Lord would call them to recognize what they were doing and move toward change. Paul picked up this theme in his epistles, challenging Christians to speak the truth in love to one another (Ephesians 4:15). From both his writings and the words of Jesus you can see the necessary balance between loving relationships and the confrontation of destructive behaviors. Membership in Christian community must involve a willingness to sensitively challenge one another to grow beyond old habits and chronic sin. Denial and "no talk" rules have no place among people gathering in Christ's name. Such dysfunctional ways lead only to destruction and death. Only in genuine community can you discover the aspects of your personality hidden and undeveloped. By having a healthy connection with people who are courageous enough to confront you, personal growth can be lovingly called forth and nurtured.

Christian community can be a powerful tool in self-discovery. It can be a place where you can learn about your grace-given identity in Christ, a truth that has the power both to transform and set you free. As those closest to you lovingly challenge the behaviors based in your old sinful nature, you can be inspired to mature in the Christ-like qualities present deep within your spirit. By forcing you to face up to sin honestly, in an atmosphere of grace and patience, the Christian community is faithfully fulfilling its call to help you become more and more like Jesus. While not easy, such confrontation is in fact a blessing that will reap a great harvest of change in your life, if you will allow it.

A Committed Community

Jesus left no question about the level of commitment necessary to be part of His community. If someone was going to join, he needed to come wholeheartedly or not at all. In Luke 14 He told His followers that they needed to count the cost before saying yes to Him, for being His disciple was not without risk.

If anyone comes to me and does not hate his father and mother, his wife and children, his brothers

117

*and sisters—yes, even his own life — he cannot be my
disciple. And anyone who does not carry his cross and
follow me cannot be my disciple.*

*Suppose one of you wants to build a tower. Will he
not first sit down and estimate the cost to see if he has
enough money to complete it? For if he lays the foundation and is not able to finish it, everyone who sees it
will ridicule him, saying, "This fellow began to build
and was not able to finish."*

*Or suppose a king is about to go to war against
another king. Will he not first sit down and consider
whether he is able with ten thousand men to oppose
one coming against him with twenty thousand? If he is
not able, he will send a delegation while the other is
still a long way off and will ask for terms of peace. In
the same way, any of you who does not give up everything he has cannot become my disciple.*

— Luke 14:28-33

The Lord's disciples did not float in and out of His community at will. The Gospels reveal that they stayed together
through the good and the bad, when following Him was
popular, and when it meant the potential for personal harm.
Granted, they all reacted and ran at His arrest, but at Pentecost they were all there waiting and watching for what was
to come. (Except Judas, of course.) They were committed!

If community is to work as intended, you and every other
member must be committed to see it through to the end.
Whether it is an eight week experiment or a long term journey, being faithful to being there is very important. Change
is not a result of occasional "blasts" of power from the Holy
Spirit. It is the result of a long term process of showing up
prepared to participate. It is the fruit of daily placing one
foot in front of the other in pursuit of Christ's embrace, confident that every member is there alongside you. It is, in
truth, not a place for the fickle or faint-hearted. If community is to work, you and those gathered together with you
must be willing to be at your posts faithfully and reliably.

Such levels of commitment foster deeper levels of consecration and involvement all around.

A Celebrating Community

The final ingredient necessary to healthy community is a spirit of celebration. It is one of the distinguishing marks of truly being the people of Christ. The first century Christian community gathered at least once a week to hold a celebration. Though they lived in a world hostile to their faith, these early believers were marked by what Peter called "an inexpressible and glorious joy." And that joy overflowed into the society in which they lived, attracting people to the way of Jesus Christ.

You and I know that life is not without difficulty, trial and suffering. On this side of eternity things can be tough, very tough. But like the early church, you must choose to be part of Christ's celebrating community, ready at a moment's notice to throw a party in Jesus' name.

There are three qualities essential to such celebrations. First, the community should be worshipful, caught up through songs, scripture and testimony with the wonder of God. You are to declare the glory of His greatness and majesty. Secondly, there should be a deep sense of gratitude. Through Christ, each member has received grace upon grace from God, undeserved and without strings. God has simply been so good! And thirdly, each celebration should be a declaration of hope. In spite of the ups and downs life brings, you and your community can declare with confidence that "all things do work for good" (Romans 8:28). Regardless of the chaos, on the other side are even greater experiences of God's loving embrace.

Christian community is an essential part of your journey to God's embrace. I encourage you to find that group of fellow travelers who will link arms with you along the journey to the Father's house of love. If you are already experiencing such a shared life, bless and nurture it more and more. If you are not yet part of such a group, begin to "ask, seek and knock" in search of that place today. Pray, enlisting the Holy Spirit's help in connecting you with those special people who will be used of God to change your life forever.

Questions For Discussion And Review

1. What first comes to your mind when you read that community is an essential part of the journey to God's embrace?

2. What did Brennan Manning mean by the "Jesus and me mentality"?

3. What ingredients of community can you identify in Acts 2:42-47?

4. Read 1 John 4:19-21. Put what John is saying into your own words.

5. What do you believe to be essential to true Christian community?

6. Briefly define the following characteristics of true community.

7. A called-out community.

8. A called-together community.

9. A Christ-centered community.

10. A compassionate community.

11. A caring community.

12. A confessing community.

13. A confrontational community.

14. A committed community.

15. A celebrating community.

16. If you were to start such a community, how would you begin?

17. What impact do you believe community could have upon your journey to God's embrace?

Chapter Seven

God Invites You
Into His Embrace

What if God made you the same offer that He did Solomon? How would you respond? Solomon followed his father David as King of Israel (1 Kings 3). The Bible tells us that in the first days of his reign, he dearly loved the Lord. On one occasion, Solomon went to the high places of Gibeon to honor God with sacrifices. There he offered one thousand burnt offerings on the altar as a sign of his love and devotion.

The following night, God appeared to Solomon in a dream and said, "Ask for whatever you want me to give you." As you know, Solomon asked for wisdom in order that he could properly discern right from wrong. The Lord granted his request, and throughout the centuries Solomon has been known as the wisest man who ever lived.

If the Lord appeared to you tonight in a dream and offered you the same opportunity, what would you want? It would be wise if you took some time to think this over. What you ask for may reveal a great deal about the deepest desires of your heart.

There was a time when I may have requested perfect health or wealth or unusual spiritual insight. I certainly could have built a case that these things would help me better serve the Lord. I have a friend who is tired of being alone and longing to find that special someone. There would be a real desire for him to ask for a godly spouse. I know several couples who desperately want children and would probably ask God for a family. In fact, there may be any one of a myriad of good and legitimate things you may desire. But, what *should* you request?

In considering this hypothetical offer, I remember being told that "good things are the enemy of the best thing." Why? Because good things never adequately satisfy the deepest hunger of the human heart. I've lived long enough to see healthy, wealthy and powerful people deeply discontented and broken. And we all know marriage is not always a pain-less endeavor for couples. And for some, children can be-come a source of great heartache and pain. Not one of these many good things comes with a guarantee of bringing the ultimate fulfillment and satisfaction we long for in life. In fact, they were never intended to be our source of ultimate contentment.

What then is the very best thing God can offer you? As I am sure you suspect by now, it is the blessing of daily mak-ing the journey to His embrace. His embrace is the all-sur-passing gift of His grace, able to bring rest and quiet to your inmost being. Growing closer to the Lord, sensing the won-der of His presence, soaking in His love, being passionate for Christ and fellowshiping with the Holy Spirit have no equal. Thus, the pursuit of God's embrace is unquestion-ably the "best thing" you could ever have in life.

After all, you were made for this intimacy. Look at Adam and Eve before the fall and you see an indescribable oneness and harmony with God. Fully aware of His presence, they were even able to hear the Lord walking through the gar-den. He was ever present and they were always aware that their God was close at hand. Their experience was supposed to be your experience but, as you know, sin got in the way. Yet God, unsatisfied with the separation sin caused, sent Jesus to pay every penalty of your rebellion so you might be united once again with your Heavenly Father. Christ's blood has made oneness and harmony possible, a priceless sacrifice for your reunion. God knew you would be broken and unfulfilled without Him, and so He gave His only Son for your salvation. Therefore, intimacy with God is the one request that stands above all others.

God Invites You To
An Intimate Relationship With Him

While the situation I have presented is hypothetical, the potential for growing in relationship with the Triune God is most real. Jesus repeatedly said that you need only ask for something in His name, and God would move into action (John14:13). But, you must ask. You need to welcome God's activity in and upon your life. It is yours to petition Him to move you ever closer to His embrace.

God is not going to force this purpose upon you, or make you one with Him whether you want it or not. He does not intrude. He invites. Your Heavenly Father has made every provision necessary for experiencing harmony with His children. But He never imposes such a relationship on anyone. He does beckon you to open your heart to His presence. But He never bullies. You are welcomed to respond to Him by asking the Father to do whatever is necessary in drawing you into His arms. God longs to empower you for such a journey toward intimacy. Will you cry out and say, "Dear Father, above everything that life affords, this is what I want most of all! Please draw me closer to You."

Are You Hungry Enough To Seek Him?

In the introduction to his classic volume, *The Pursuit of God*, Tozer wrote that there is an ever-increasing number of people hungry for God. According to Tozer, such people want more than sound doctrine, good sermons and right teaching. They want the "inner sweetness" of God Himself, and long to delight regularly in His presence. Though written decades ago, the insights and discernment of A. W. Tozer are as relevant and accurate today as they were when he first penned those thoughts. Countless people are worn out by religion, yet desperate for more of God.

Tozer assured his readers that intimacy with God was possible for every believer and he encouraged them to pursue God above all else. He wrote,

> The man who has God for his treasure has all things in one. Many ordinary treasures may be denied him, or if he is allowed to have them, the enjoyment of them will be so tempered that they will never be necessary to his happiness. Or if he must see them go, one after one, he will scarcely feel a sense of loss, for having the source of all things he has in One all satisfaction, all pleasure and delight. Whatever he may lose he has actually lost nothing, for he now has it all in One, and he has it purely, legitimately and forever.[29]

Are you numbered among the hungry and thirsty people Tozer writes about? Do you long for the satisfaction and delight that comes in pursuing the Treasure above all others? Are you willing to lose even important things to gain more of God? Has dissatisfaction with your walk with God ignited a passion to know Him more? I believe the answer to each question is a resounding "Yes!"

But the desire of your heart is to be translated into action. I encourage you to go before God, asking Him to draw you into His loving presence, not for a moment, but as an ongoing experience of life. I assure you that He will hear that prayer and act upon your request. But will you, in turn, faithfully respond by actively and daily pursuing His intimate embrace above all else? If and when you do, you should get ready for a journey, not of a lifetime, but of all time and beyond.

Questions For Discussion And Review

1. Is the journey to God's embrace more important than all else that life affords? If so, why? If not, explain your response.

2. Why does God invite people into intimacy with Him and not force them to love Him?

3. What did Tozer mean when he said that "The man who has God for his treasure has all things in one"?

4. How do you intend to incorporate the principles of this book into your daily life?

5. Lay out a plan of action for accomplishing the above.

Selected Bibliography

A'Kempis, Thomas, *Of the Imitation of Christ*. Whitaker House, 1981.

Bickle, Mike, *Passion for Jesus*. Orlando: Creation House, 1993.

Brown, Stephen, *Approaching God*. Nashville: Moorings, 1996.

de Caussade, Jean-Pierre, *Sacrament of the Present Moment*. San Francisco: Harper Collins, 1989.

Fenelon, Francois, *The Seeking Heart*. Beaumont, Texas: Seed Sowers, 1992.

Fitz-Gibbon, Andy and Jane, *The Kiss of Intimacy*. Crowborough: Monarch, 1995.

Foster, Richard, *Celebration of Discipline*. Harper San Francisco, 1988.

_____, *Prayer: Finding the Hearts True Home*. San Francisco, California: Harper, 1992.

Gire, Ken, *Windows of the Soul*. Grand Rapids: Zondervan Publishing House, 1996.

Guyon, Jeanne, *Experiencing the Depths of Jesus Christ*, Seed Sowers, 1975.

Hallesby, Ole, *Prayer*, Augsburg Fortress, 1994.

Lord, Peter, *Hearing God*, Baker Book House, 1988.

Manning, Brennan, *The Signature of Jesus*, Sisters, Oregon: Multnomah. 1988.

Merton, Thomas, *No Man Is an Island*, Harcourt Brace Jovanivich, New York 1983.

Mulholland, Robert, *Shaped by the Word*, The Upper Room, 1985.

_____, *Invitation to a Journey*, Inter-Varsity Press, 1993.

Muto, Susan, *Late Have I Loved Thee*, New York: Crossroads. 1995.

Nouwen, Henri, *Life of the Beloved*, New York: Crossroads, 1992.

_____, *Return of the Prodigal Son*, Image Books, 1994.

_____, *The Inner Voice of Love*, New York: Doubleday, 1996.

_____, *The Way of the Heart*, Harper San Francisco, 1991.

Smith, James Bryan, *Embracing the Love of God*, Harper, San Francisco, 1995.

St. John of the Cross, *Dark Night of the Soul*, Image, 1990.

Tirabassi, Becky, *Let Prayer Change Your Life*, Oliver-Nelson Books, 1990 and 1992.

Tuoti, Frank, *Why Not Be a Mystic*, New York: Crossroads. 1996.

Tozer, A. W., *The Pursuit of God*, Camp Hill: Christian Publications, Inc., 1982.

Willard, Dallas, *The Spirit of the Disciplines*, New York: Harper and Row, 1988.

Endnotes

[1] I have written far more extensively about this time in my book, *Draw Close To the Fire: How to Find God in the Darkness*, Grand Rapids; Chosen, 1998

[2] Guyon, Jeanne, *Experiencing the Depths of Jesus Christ*. Seed Sowers. pp. X , XI.22

[3] Tozer, A. W., *The Pursuit of God*, Camp Hill, Pa., Christian Publications, 1982 p. 10

[4] *The Pursuit of God*, p. 15

[5] Tuoti, Frank. *Why Not Be a Mystic*, New York, Crossroads. 1995, p.158

[6] Manning, Brennan. *The Signature of Jesus*, Sisters, Oregon, Multnomah. 1988, p. 214, 215

[7] Manning, p. 93

[8] Brown, Stephen, *Approaching God*, Nashville, Moorings, 1996, p. 3

[9] This quote comes from a book titled *Practicing His Presence*, a combined volume of works by Frank Laubach and Brother Lawrence. It is made available by Seed Sowers Publishers, Beaumont Texas, p. 36, 37

[10] These "I will" statements are taken from Ezekiel 34-36.

[11] de Caussade, Jean-Pierre, *The Sacrament of the Present Moment*, Harper San Francisco, p. 18

[12] *Ibid.*, p. 44

[13] Foster, Richard, *Prayer: Finding the Heart's True Home*, Harper San Francisco. 1992, p. 20, 21

[14] Guyon, *Experiencing the Depths of Jesus Christ*, p. 27

[15] *Ibid.*, p. 28, 29

[16] de Caussade, Jean-Pierre, *The Sacrament of the Present Moment*, Harper San Francisco, 1995, p. 93

[17] For a far more detailed treatment of this subject, see my book, *Draw Close to the Fire*

[18] These principles have been gleaned from *The Dark Night of the Soul*, by St. John of the Cross, published in New York by Doubleday, in 1990

[19] Foster, p. 22

[20] Nouwen, Henri, *Here and Now*, New York, Crossroads. 1995, p. 39

[21] Gire, Kenneth, *Windows of the Soul*, Zondervan, 1996, p. 17

[22] Tirabassi, Becky, *Let Prayer Change Your Life*, Oliver Nelson Books, 1992, pp. 60-61

[23] *Ibid.*, p. 61

[24] Tuoti, p.131 It is important to know that Tuoti's definition of "mystical knowledge" is " a personal experience of the living God," and is therefore not repugnant to the evangelical Christian community. He is not forwarding a notion of some mindless irrational encounter with the supernatural or nirvana-like state of consciousness. He writes that, "All genuine Christian mysticism must be grounded in sound theology lest it run the risk of being a self-styled kind of counterfeit mysticism." p.23

[25] Mulholland, Robert, *Invitation to a Journey*, IVP 1993, p. 12

[26] Tuoti, p. 65

[27] Mulholland, Robert, *Shaped by the Word*, IVP, p.148, 149

[28] Manning, Brennan, *The Signature of Jesus*, Sisters, Oregon, Multnomah 1988 p. 122, 123

[29] Tozer, A. W., *The Pursuit of God*, Christian Publications, 1982, p. 19, 20

The Sandberg
Leadership Center

On the Campus of Ashland Theological Seminary

*Don't do what the world needs
Do what keeps you alive;
For what the world needs
Is you, alive!*
— Howard Thurman

The Sandberg Leadership Center is located on the Campus of Ashland Theological Seminary. From the heart of northeast Ohio, the center serves the growing need for quality leadership training throughout the United States.

Leadership is at a time of transition. The "hero-leader" of the past is no longer adequate for the relational world of the new century. Before there can be real change in our institutions, there must be change in our understanding and practice of leadership.

Our Mission

We are a center of transformational learning, committed to the spiritual and character formation of servant leaders

135

who will make a difference in business, government, church, and society.

We practice transformational learning...
Transformational learning produces reflective leaders of integrity, courage and wisdom.

We commit to spiritual and character formation...
Leaders express clear, personal core values in competencies consistent with good leadership.

We believe servant leaders make a difference...
Leadership is the ability to get things done. Servant leadership accomplishes tasks by investing in people.

We serve leaders in business, government, church and society.
The Center will focus on developing leadership in business, government, church and society.

Our Values

The Leadership Center is committed to a biblical understanding of life, education, and ministry:

- We value **servant leadership** as the biblical model.

- We value **spiritual formation** that results in life renewed and the recovery of identity in Christ.

- We value **self-understanding** and **discovery**.

- We value **team building** and shared responsibility within the organization.

- We value the vision of the leader as a **change agent** in the organization and society.

- We value Christian **witness** and **mission**.
- We value **academic excellence.**

- We value the **redemption, personal healing** and **equipping** of each participant.

- We value an attitude of **stewardship** and a careful **discernment of the culture.**

Seeing The Future, Now

The decades of changing culture have shaken the foundations of business, government and the church. The older ways of management treat the church, business and government as machines. The new paradigm, formed through servant leadership, views organization in personal images of teams, networks and partners or in biblical images of "family," "body" and "living stones."

Transition is traumatic. There are loud voices from the "not too distant past" calling for structures that stifle creativity and diminish the energy of relationships. Yet, there is a still voice from the "not too distant future" that longs for leadership. But, it is not necessarily a cry for more leaders, or better leaders, but a cry for a different kind of leader: one who is empowered by the synergy of servant leadership and spiritual formation in renewing the organization on a True Foundation.

Such a leader is competent in two skills:

- **The forming of self as servant leader.**
- **The forming of the organization as servant people.**

This leader is equipped to move the organization toward a system of relationship and empowerment. It is our purpose at The Sandberg Leadership Center to model the new paradigm as we provide transformational learning for Christian leaders in business, government and the church.

Contact Us

If we can serve you in leadership training; if you would like information on programs available for you and your organization; or if you would like to know how you can participate in the development of The Sandberg Leadership Center, contact us at:

The Sandberg Leadership Center
910 Center Street
Ashland, Ohio   44805

Email: LeadOn@ashland.edu

1-419-289-5909

Richard L. Parrott, Ph.D.
Executive Director
April 2, 2000